THE LAND OF ORANGE GROVES AND JAILS

UPTON SINCLAIR'S CALIFORNIA

"Kudos to Coodley for shedding light on a rich sampling of the life and work of a great American patriot. An engaging, interesting, well-researched, and well-done book."
—MICHAEL PARENTI, AUTHOR OF Superpatriotism and
The Assassination of Julius Caesar

"Seven decades after Upton Sinclair's breathtaking campaign for governor, California is a land of corporate orange groves and countless jails. In this meticulous book, Lauren Coodley provides context and excerpts that blow away fog about Upton Sinclair—a terrific writer and committed activist who broke down barriers everywhere he turned, and one of the most brilliant American polemicists of the twentieth century."
—NORMAN SOLOMON, AUTHOR OF The Habits of Highly Deceptive Media
AND COAUTHOR OF Target Iraq: What the News Media Didn't Tell You

THE LAND OF ORANGE GROVES AND JAILS
UPTON SINCLAIR'S CALIFORNIA

Edited by Lauren Coodley

SANTA CLARA UNIVERSITY, SANTA CLARA, CALIFORNIA
HEYDAY BOOKS, BERKELEY, CALIFORNIA

Library of Congress Cataloging-in-Publication Data

Sinclair, Upton, 1878–1968.
The land of orange groves and jails : Upton Sinclair's California / edited by Lauren Coodley.
     p. cm. – (A California legacy book)
Includes bibliographical references.
   ISBN 1-890771-95-3 (pbk. : alk. paper)
   1. Sinclair, Upton, 1878–1968—Homes and haunts—California.
2. Authors, American—Homes and haunts—California. 3. Authors, American—20th century—Biography. 4. California—Social life and customs.
5. California—Description and travel. 6. California—Biography.
I. Coodley, Lauren. II. Title. III. Series.
   PS3537.I85A6 2004
   813'.52—dc22   2004017891

Orders, inquiries, and correspondence should be addressed to:
Heyday Books
P.O. Box 9145
Berkeley, CA 94709
(510) 549-3564; Fax (510) 549-1889
heyday@heydaybooks.com

Printed by United Graphics Inc., Mattoon, IL
10 9 8 7 6 5 4 3 2 1

Contents

Acknowledgments

MY INTEREST IN Upton Sinclair began in 1995, when I showed a copy of Lyn Goldfarb's documentary about the EPIC movement, *We Have a Plan*, to a class of community college students. I was struck by how enthused the students were about the plan, and by how much we had all lost by forgetting this fiery chapter of California history.

Eventually I wrote several grant proposals toward a documentary film biography of Sinclair; my thanks to the California Council for the Humanities for their generous support. Although the film remains to be done, the grant enabled me to assemble the first reunion of Sinclair scholars held in decades, at the University of California, Los Angeles. My thanks to Bud Lesser, Ron Gottesman, Mike Riherd, Jon Yoder, Robert Hahn, Deirdre Lashgari, Woody Nance, Robert Wright, Doug Dibble, and Martin Zanger for participating in this colloquium. Their insights laid the foundation for my understanding of Upton Sinclair.

I am indebted to Sachiko Nakada for her *Japanese Empathy for Upton Sinclair* (1990) and to German scholar Dieter Herms for editing *Upton Sinclair: Literature and Social Reform* (1990). Along with Edward Allatt's work in Britain, these scholars helped me to understand the international attention that Sinclair received.

The Lilly Library awarded me an Everett Helm fellowship to work in the Sinclair archives; many thanks for the kindness of their librarians and archivists.

For their generous offer of the Mesa Refuge, I would like to thank the Common Counsel Foundation; for the infinitely helpful sources of citations and fascinating "Sinclairiana," thanks to John Ahouse; and for the warmth and passing of the flame, Robert and Genevieve Hahn. Thanks to JJ Wilson for being not only my first but also my best teacher. Thanks to Dana Gioia for bringing Upton Sinclair and me to Heyday. Keni Drost, Keni Kent, and Jeannine Gendar gave me thoughtful editorial input, and my children have been a constant source of encouragement: many thanks to all of you.

Upton Sinclair concluded his *Autobiography* this way: "I don't know whether anyone will care to examine my heart, but if they do they will find two words there—Social Justice." This book is dedicated to two people who brought Sinclair's words to life: Tillie Olsen and Paul Wellstone.

Introduction

UPTON SINCLAIR (1878–1968) is famous, but not for his life in California. Most Americans know him simply as the author of *The Jungle*, the astonishing novel that rocked the beginning of the twentieth century with its exposé of contamination in the meat-packing industry. California history textbooks mention Upton Sinclair only in passing reference to what they usually label as his "unsuccessful" campaign for governor in 1934. But it is, in fact, impossible to understand Upton Sinclair without reference to his life in California, and it is equally incomplete to think about California in the twentieth century without turning to Upton Sinclair's work.

Describing the 1920s, Carey McWilliams wrote, "For Southern California the decade was a long drunken orgy, one protracted debauch."[1] Having arrived in California in 1915, Upton Sinclair settled amidst this "drunken orgy" and proceeded to chronicle it mercilessly, tirelessly, and with great delight. That delight is one of the fascinating contradictions of Upton Sinclair, whose life, a reporter for the *Los Angeles Times* recently said, was "as compelling as his writing."[2] With the dedication of the Liberty Hill Monument in 1998, the republication of *The Brass Check* and *The Millennium* in 2002, the first annual "Uppie Awards" held in San Pedro in May 2003, and the encore performance of Chapter One of *Oil!* by Word for Word Theater Company in San Francisco in fall 2003, Sinclair's life and works are blooming once more into California's consciousness. As California faces new assaults on free speech, labor organizing, food safety, the natural environment, and the teaching of history, Sinclair has perhaps never been as relevant as he is right now.

In 1999, media critic Norman Solomon wrote, "The next time you wonder about the beef on your plate, you might think of Upton Sinclair and ask yourself why it's still such a media jungle out there."[3] When ABC reporters went undercover in 1997 in meat-handling jobs and hid cameras in wigs to record filthy food practices, jurors called it fraud and fined them $5.5 million. The *San Francisco Chronicle* condemned this verdict, noting that "undercover reporting is a proud tradition that dates back to Upton Sinclair" and asking, "Who will tell the people the truth?"[4]

Californians are stunned by the speed of change of the last hundred years and Upton Sinclair waits patiently to explain when and how these changes happened. He can tell us about Hollywood and how it became an industrialized dream machine; he can tell us about oil, and how it created the freeways that destroyed the railroads, and the subdivisions that destroyed the orchards. He can tell us, perhaps most importantly, about the events that other historians avoided or forgot. One of these events was the effort to defend four women radicals, arrested in San Bernardino in 1929, in the story which gives us the title of this book. It was the Industrial Workers of the World, the Wobblies, who called California the "land of orange groves and jails," this land that drew workers of all colors like magnets to a file with its promise of oranges like gold in the streets. This was the place where the Wobbly dream died, defeated in a bitter port struggle in Long Beach, depicted in Sinclair's play *Singing Jailbirds*. He wrote it in a white heat of desperation to tell the world what was happening to these longshoremen, while most artists of the twenties were too busy to notice.

From Sinclair's film of *The Jungle*, made in 1915, to MGM's film of his novel *The Wet Parade* and Disney's 1962 film of *The Gnomobile*, Upton Sinclair wrestled with Hollywood, using it, used by it, emerging from each encounter charged with more ferocity and a determination to win with his pen what would be denied him at the ballot box.

The success of Sinclair's World's End spy series in arousing his readers to join the European war against Hitler has barely been recognized. With this series, which absorbed Sinclair throughout the 1940s and gained him admirers from Britain to Japan to Germany, he received again the worldwide acclaim which he had first earned when he went into the stockyards in 1905 to examine how cattle were slaughtered.

Arriving in California at the age of thirty-seven, Sinclair stayed for fifty years, leaving only at the very end of his life, in 1965. In those fifty years, California was transformed, and Sinclair became one of its chroniclers, its visionaries, and its foremost activists. He had already gone through a number of transformations before his arrival. He had survived his father's alcoholism, his mother's poverty. He had grabbed what crumbs of education were available to him, and as a sensitive young man, he had searched for the source of the injustices that doomed his own household and the lives that surrounded it. He had discovered first poetry, then religion, then socialism.

Along with Jack London, he had founded the Intercollegiate Socialist Society in 1905, determined that if "the professors refuse to teach the students about modern life, it was up to the students to teach themselves."[5] By the time Sinclair moved to California, Jack London was dead, a victim of alcohol, along with so many of Sinclair's closest friends. Almost alone among his male contemporaries, Sinclair was determined not to waste his life in brawling, womanizing, and hard drinking.[6] By 1913 he had discovered the secrets of health, the sanity of monogamy, and the importance of publicly facing down the industrial giants of turn-of-the-century America.

Sinclair had survived his undercover life in Packingtown documenting the horrors of the slaughterhouse; he had survived the arson of his utopian community in New Jersey, and the disintegration of his first marriage. Struggling with his health, he had gone to the Battle Creek Sanitarium run by William Kellogg, where he had met and courted Mary Craig. This former "southern belle," as she sardonically called herself, would remain his wife and best friend until her death in 1961.[7]

With Mary Craig he came to California; they settled in the Southland: tennis with Henry Ford, hiking with Charlie Chaplin, psychic experiments with Albert Einstein, correspondence daily with everyone from Margaret Sanger to George Bernard Shaw. Sinclair's first biographer, Floyd Dell, described him at the age of forty-five as "a slight, wiry, graying figure, an excellent tennis player, an eager talker, wearing the cast-off clothes of a rich young friend…boyish, impulsive, trustful, stubborn, fondly regarded as impractical by those who love him."[8]

Seen as a crackpot by those comfortable with injustice, seen as a gentle charmer by those who detested his politics, raising his voice at Liberty Hill to thunder the Bill of Rights to striking Wobblies, or absorbed by the arguments over oil fields in Long Beach, Sinclair worked at his life, assiduously, ardently, tending his friendships, his roses, his typewriter in the garden. Cannery organizer Dorothy Healey said of Sinclair:

> I never met him, heard him speak, or worked for him. When he ran for governor on the EPIC platform, I was languishing in a jail in Imperial Valley. But I read him, and *Oil!* and *King Coal* charted the rest of my life for me.[9]

Lifelong activist Lorna Smith titled her only published work "My Life Was Changed by Upton Sinclair."[10] Her father had told her, "When you go into a meat market and see the government seal on a quarter of beef, you will know it's there because of Upton Sinclair." She went to the library, got the book, and later wrote, "His quotation 'I aimed at their hearts and hit their stomachs' did not apply to me. He hit my heart." Smith wrote to Sinclair and he responded. She established an EPIC club in her Glendale home and left her church when it would not speak up for Sinclair. Later, after she marched for civil rights with Stokely Carmichael, she said, "Sinclair wrote to me, saying he had not known I was down in Mississippi, and he honored me for it."[11]

The Sinclair Archives are at the Lilly Library, in Indiana; California's Huntington Library rejected them because of his politics.[12] Ronald Gottesman, who inventoried the archives, described Sinclair as "a paradigm of hope,"[13] and indeed Sinclair epitomized what historian Kevin Starr calls California's "ache of promise."[14] In his fifty years here, Sinclair brought muckraking to a high art, with the first examinations of the California press, the schools, and the colleges, and with early, experimental, agit-prop theater. His life was a play with many acts, many scenes, including a children's fantasy about saving the redwoods in the 1930s, an eleven-volume antifascist spy series in the 1940s, and in between, a jaw-dropping campaign for governor of his adopted state that brought popular culture into the heart of electoral politics.

This volume gives us a chance to look closely at what Sinclair saw and did in California. It is divided metaphorically into the rooms of his house: his political awakenings, both physical and mental; his earliest impressions of California as a traveler and an activist; his complex struggles with Hollywood; and his courageous and unconventional attempt to "End Poverty in California." In California, Sinclair's attention to health, to friendship, to labor, and to nature could be integrated, and he could emerge from the haunting scenes of his earlier eastern life fully himself and fully engaged. His holistic vision, quintessentially Californian, flourished in a land whose own essence ranged so eclectically from orange groves to jails.

Notes

1. Carey McWilliams, *Southern California: An Island on the Land* (Santa Barbara, Calif.: Peregrine Smith, 1973)

2. Cecilia Rasmussen, "Muckraker's Own Life as Compelling as His Writing," *Los Angeles Times*, May 11, 2003

3. Norman Solomon, *San Francisco Bay Guardian*, July 1999

4. *San Francisco Chronicle*, "Killing the Messenger," January 26, 1997, B4

5. Upton Sinclair, *American Outpost* (New York: Farrar and Rinehart, 1932), 159. The idea was Sinclair's, but the society was organized with Jack London as president because of his enormous popularity with students.

6. See Louis Henry Hughes, who contrasts Sinclair to other twentieth-century American novelists in *Uppie Speaks* 2:8, September 1978, 3.

7. Sinclair's wife continued to be known as Mary Craig after their marriage.

8. Floyd Dell, *Upton Sinclair: A Study in Social Protest* (New York: George Doran, 1927), 186

9. Interview with Dorothy Healey by Robert Hahn, "Upton Sinclair Newsletter" 1:3, October 1990

10. Lorna Smith, "My Life Was Changed by Upton Sinclair," *The Upton Beall Sinclair Centenary Journal* 1:1, September 1978, 1

11. Ibid., 2

12. When Sinclair offered his papers to the Huntington Library in 1956, the chairman of the board was Herbert Hoover, and so, Sinclair wrote, "I was not favored by the Pasadena gentlemen who control the Huntington Library." (Upton Sinclair, *The Autobiography of Upton Sinclair*, New York: Harcourt Brace and World, 1962, 304).

13. Ronald Gottesman, "A Paradigm of Hope," unpublished speech, October 1978

14. Kevin Starr, *Americans and the California Dream* (New York: Oxford University Press, 1973), viii

Upton Sinclair was born on September 20, 1878, in Baltimore, Maryland, where he grew up in a series of boardinghouses.

One
"Like the Falling Down of Prison Walls": Political Awakenings

If the public thinks of me as a muckraker exclusively, it is not
because of the limitation of my mind but of the public's mind.
— *Upton Sinclair to Lewis Mumford, December 1, 1926*

SINCLAIR WAS INDEED a "muckraker," but his work would tran-
scend that label. Describing his first encounters with socialism, he
wrote of his amazement that, "after all these years...I did not have
to carry the whole burden of humanity's future upon my two frail
shoulders."[1] At twenty-four years old, he began his lifetime project
of sharing this insight with Americans and his international reader-
ship. *The Jungle* was published in 1906, when he was twenty-eight.
His first publication in California was a pioneering anthology of pro-
letarian literature, *The Cry for Justice*, a collection of five thousand
works of poetry, philosophy, and fiction. He dedicated the book to
"those unknown ones, who by their dimes and quarters keep the
socialist movement going."[2]

As is evident in the following selections, for Sinclair, the personal
was indeed political. This conviction was derived partly from temperance marches with his mother: part of Sinclair's political analysis was
that a healthy and sober personal life would allow more time and
space for social activism, and unlike many writers and activists of the
twentieth century, he rejected the use of alcohol.[3] Sinclair's friendships
with powerful woman activists throughout his life also contributed.

Sinclair at twenty-seven, while writing *The Jungle*. In 1904, the editor of
Appeal to Reason commissioned Sinclair to write a series of articles exposing
conditions in Chicago slaughterhouses. "I set out for Chicago and for
seven weeks lived among the wage slaves of the Beef Trust," he later said
in his autobiography.

Particularly influential was Charlotte Perkins Gilman, the California
sociologist. Sinclair's own utopian colony, Helicon Hall, was based
on her vision of cooperative housework and childcare.[4]

Sinclair came to California for his health, which had been a constant source of concern to him. In 1909 he wrote, "I look about me
in the world and nearly everybody I know is sick. I could name one
after another a hundred men and women who are doing vital work
for progress and carrying a cruel handicap of physical suffering."[5]
Sinclair concluded that health problems prevented many activists
from fully devoting themselves to movements for social change. In
1920, he wrote *The Book of Life* to guide his working-class readers,
extolling the benefits of yogurt, vegetables, and exercise. The new

fields of feminist and cultural history can help us contextualize this aspect of Sinclair, who, writes critic William Bloodworth, represents "an unusually vigorous attempt to combine questions of food with political propaganda."[6]

It is interesting that Upton Sinclair, who was willing to go to jail in support of labor and free speech issues, has been ridiculed continuously since his death for being a "bluenose": a person with strongly puritanical moral convictions; one who believes that having a good time is immoral; an ultraconservative.[7] Recent scholarship on the history of masculinity and the political implications of personal life choices could alter the framework within which we interpret Sinclair's life.[8]

Notes

1. Upton Sinclair, *American Outpost* (New York: Farrar and Rinehart Inc., 1932), 143

2. Upton Sinclair, *The Cry for Justice* (New York and Pasadena: Upton Sinclair, 1915), 2

3. See Robin Room, "A Reverence for Strong Drink: The Lost Generation and the Elevation of Alcohol in American Culture," *Journal of Studies on Alcohol* 45:6, 1980.

4. Helicon Hall was Sinclair's effort to set up a cooperative colony in New Jersey in 1907. It was destroyed in a mysterious arson fire less than one year after it began.
   Regarding Charlotte Perkins Gilman, see Carl Degler's introduction to her *Women and Economics* (New York: Harper Torchbooks, 1966). See also Ann J. Lane, *To Herland and Beyond: The Life and Work of Charlotte Perkins Gilman* (New York: Pantheon, 1995). Sinclair often suggested that people interested in utopian societies read Gilman's books.

5. Upton Sinclair, *Good Health and How We Won It* (New York: Frederick Stokes, 1909), cited in William Bloodworth, "From *The Jungle* to the Fasting Cure," *Journal of Americn Culture* II, Fall 1979, no page noted

6. Bloodworth, "*The Jungle* to the Fasting Cure," 442

7. Upton Sinclair, *The Autobiography of Upton Sinclair* (New York: Harcourt Brace and World, 1962), 248

8. Recent work on masculinity includes Gail Bederman, *Manliness and Civilization: A Cultural History of Gender and Race in the United States* (Chicago: University of Chicago, 1995) and Michael Kimmel, *Manhood in America* (New York: Free Press, 1996).

Youth

from *American Outpost: A Book of Reminiscences*, 1932

As THE ADULT CHILD of an alcoholic, Upton Sinclair was almost alone among his radical colleagues in refusing to drink. Sinclair's choice of temperance as a political issue is one of the many aspects of his life which demand historical reevaluation. He was born into a household deeply affected by temperance reformers such as Frances Willard.[1] As the feminist son of an alcoholic, he continued to support the Eighteenth Amendment, even as sentiment for its repeal increased in the twenties. Through his novel and film *The Wet Parade* (1931, 1932), he persisted in raising an issue that many of his contemporaries dismissed as old-fashioned and prudish.

Today this political analysis of the effects of alcohol has been largely forgotten, and the efforts of the feminist reformers who sought to ban liquor have long been regarded with contempt and amusement. Yet Sinclair continued to insist that the welfare of women and children was, as Willard argued, vitally affected by alcoholism, and he backed his ideas up with action. As late as 1954, in *The Cup of Fury*, he wrote, "I cast my vote against social drinking. I will not keep a dog in my house that bites one out of every five or nine people that stoops to pet it. Nor will I sanction alcohol because it harms one out of every five or nine that drink it."[2]

Notes

1. See Ruth Bordin, *Frances Willard: A Biography* (Chapel Hill, N.C.: University of North Carolina, 1986), as well as Carolyn De Swarte Gifford, *Writing Out My Heart: Selections from the Journal of Frances Willard, 1855–96* (University of Illinois Press, 1995).

2. Upton Sinclair's *The Cup of Fury* (Great Neck, N.Y.: Channel Press, 1956) became a surprise best-seller for a small publisher of religious books.

M Y POOR FATHER was no longer in position to qualify as an educator of youth. Every year he was gripped more tightly in the claws of his Demon. He would disappear for days, and it would be my task to go and seek him in the bar-rooms which he frequented. I would find him, and there would be a moral battle. I would argue and plead and threaten; he would weep, or try to assert his authority—though I cannot recall that he ever even pretended to be angry with me. I would lead him up the street, and every corner saloon would be a new contest. "I must have just one more drink, son. I can't go home without one more. If you only knew what I am suffering!"

I would get him to bed, and hide his trousers so that he could not escape, and mother would make cups of strong black coffee, or perhaps a drink of warm water and mustard. It was the life of millions of women in those days of the American saloon; and my friend Mencken is unable to imagine why those women should have been turned into raging viragos, so displeasing to the urbane and esthetic. But believe me, I know; and so long as the memory lives in their souls, those women will go to the polls by millions and break the hearts of the "wets." The Prohibition question was settled for our time when the women of America got the ballot.

Later on, things grew worse yet. My father would no longer be found in his old haunts; he would be ashamed for his friends to see him, and would wander away. I would seek him in the dives on the Bowery—the "Highway of Lost Men," as I called it in *Love's Pilgrimage*. I would walk for hours, peering into scores of places, and at last I would find him, sunk into a chair or sleeping with his arms on a beer-soaked table. Once I found him literally in the gutter—no uncommon sight in those days.

I would get a cab and take him—no longer home, for we could not handle him; he would be delirious, and there would be need of strong-armed attendants and leather straps and iron bars. I would take him to St. Vincent's Hospital, and there, with crucified saviors looking down on us, I would pay twenty-five dollars to a silent, black-clad nun, and my father would be entered in the books and led away, quaking with terror, by a young Irish husky in white ducks. A week or two later he would emerge, weak and unsteady, pasty of complexion but full of moral fervor. He would join the church, sign pledges, vote for Sunday closing, weep on my shoulder and tell me how he loved me. For a week or a month or possibly several months he would struggle to build up his lost business and pay his debts.

————

My "LIBERAL" FRIENDS who read the manuscript of *The Wet Parade* found it sentimental, and out of the spirit of the time. To them I made answer that the experiences of my childhood, and of my wife's in the far South, were "reality," quite as much so as the blood and guts of the Chicago stockyards, or the birth-scene in *Love's Pilgrimage*. It is a fact that I have been all my life gathering material on the subject of the liquor problem. I know it with greater intimacy than any other theme I have ever handled. The list of drunkards I have wrestled with is longer than the list of coal miners, oil magnates, politicians, or any other group I have portrayed in my books.

The experiences with my father lasted thirty years; and during this period there were several uncles and cousins, and numerous friends of the family, Southern gentlemen, Northern businessmen, and even one or two of their wives. Later on, I ran into the same problem in the literary and Socialist worlds: George Sterling, Jack London, Ambrose Bierce, W. M. Reedy, O. Henry, Eugene Debs—a long list. I have a photograph of Jack and George and the latter's wife, Carrie, taken on Jack's sail-boat on San Francisco Bay; three beautiful people, young, happy, brilliant—and all three took poison to escape the claws of John Barleycorn. Now there is a new crop of friends, whom I cannot name while they are alive. Suffice it to say, they are our best—novelists, dramatists, poets, all stumbling down the same road of misery.

Revolt
from *American Outpost: A Book of Reminiscences*, 1932

DUE TO HIS FATHER'S alcoholism, Sinclair was raised in a series of dreary boarding houses, except for brief visits to the homes of his wealthy southern relatives. The contrast between wealth and poverty made a searing impression on him. "I have one favorite theme, the contrast of the social classes...one night I would be sleeping on a vermin-ridden sofa in a lodging house, and the next night under silken coverlets in a fashioned home," he explained.[1] As a teenager, Sinclair turned first to religion and then to poetry to explore the contradictions in his life, with inconclusive results. As Michael Parenti has noted, "there is no mystification more fundamental to capitalism than the silence maintained about its own origins."[2]

After Sinclair discovered socialism, an experience he likened to prison walls falling down, he published *The Jungle* in 1906. Based on his bold idea of going undercover in the Chicago stockyards, the novel became what Jack London called "the *Uncle Tom's Cabin* of wage slavery."[3] Seven years later, Sinclair and his second wife, Mary Craig, stayed up all night grieving over the massacre of coal miners in Ludlow, Colorado. The mines were owned by the Rockefeller family. In her valuable memoir, Craig recounts:

> We must do something spectacular, Upton declared, in order to enlist the public's sympathy. As the night wore on, an idea came to him at last: we would ask a group of sympathizers to put on bands of mourning crepe in memory of the murdered women and children of Ludlow and walk up and down in front of the Rockefeller offices all day... "They will surely arrest you," I argued. "Of course they will; and this is what is needed." [4]

Sinclair understood that well-known figures would draw public attention to injustice. After Sinclair was arrested, Mary Craig found sympathizers and "more important, a dozen reporters." Picketing was common in strikes, but "so far as we knew, it was the first time it had been done on the premises. Now, when the author of *The Jungle* told the story, every reporter was scribbling diligently."[5] The Sinclairs

On April 21, 1913, this daughter of a Mississippi banker married Upton Sinclair. In his biography of Sinclair, Jon Yoder writes: "Until her death in 1961, Mary Craig was Sinclair's constant companion, providing consistent ideological support for an author whose personal life was always a large part of his writing.

had invented a brilliant method of taking protests directly to the head-quarters of the corporations, a technique that has become massively popular since their brainstorm of 1913.

Notes

1. Upton Sinclair, *The Autobiography of Upton Sinclair* (New York: Harcourt Brace and World, 1962), 9

2. Michael Parenti, *History as Mystery* (San Francisco: City Lights, 1999), 17

3. Leon Harris, *Upton Sinclair, American Rebel* (Crowell: New York, 1975), 64

4. Mary Craig Sinclair, *Southern Belle* (New York, Crown Publishers, 1957), 151

5. Ibid., 152

F LOYD DELL, contemplating his biography of myself, asked me
to explain the appearance of a social rebel in a conventional
Southern family. I thought the problem over, and reported my psy-
chology as that of a "poor relation." It had been my fate from earliest
childhood to live in the presence of wealth which belonged to others.

Let me say at once that I have no idea of blaming my relatives.
They were always kind to me; their homes were open to me, and
when I came, I was a member of the family. Nor do I mean that I
was troubled by jealousy. I mean merely that all my life I was faced
by the contrast between riches and poverty, and thereby impelled
to think and to ask questions. "Mamma, why are some children
poor and others rich? How can that be fair?" I plagued my mother's
mind with the problem, and never got any answer. Now I plague the
ruling-class apologists of the world with it, and still get no answer.

The other factor in my revolt—odd as it may seem—was the
Protestant Episcopal Church. I really took the words of Jesus seriously, and when I carried the train of Bishop Potter in a confirma-
tion ceremony in the Church of the Holy Communion, I thought
I was helping to glorify the rebel carpenter, the friend of the poor
and lowly, the symbol of human brotherhood. Later, I read in the
papers that the bishop's wife had had fifty thousand dollars' worth
of jewels stolen, and had set the police to hunting for the thief. I
couldn't understand how a bishop's wife could own fifty thousand
dollars' worth of jewels, and the fact stuck in my mind, and had a
good deal to do with the fading away of my churchly ardor.

From the age of perhaps seventeen to twenty-two, I faced our civilization of class privilege absolutely alone in my own mind; that is
to say, whatever I found wrong with this civilization, I thought that
I alone knew it, and the burden of changing it rested upon my
spirit. Such was the miracle which capitalist education had been
able to perform upon my young mind, during the eleven or twelve
years that it had charge of me. It could not keep me from realizing

that the rule of society by organized greed was an evil thing; but it managed to keep me from knowing that there was anybody else in the world who thought as I did; it managed to make me regard the current movements, Bryanism and Populism, which sought to remedy this evil, as vulgar, noisy, and beneath my cultured contempt.

I knew, of course, that there had been a Socialist movement in Europe; I had heard vaguely about Bismarck persecuting these malcontents. Also, I knew there had been dreamers and cranks who had gone off and lived in colonies, and "busted up" when they faced the practical problems of life. While emotionally in revolt against Mammon-worship, I was intellectually a perfect little snob and tory. I despised modern books without having read them, and I expected social evils to be remedied by cultured and well-mannered gentlemen who had been to college and acquired noble ideals. That is as near as I can come to describing the jumble of notions I had acquired by combining John Ruskin with Godkin of the *New York Evening Post,* and Shelley with Dana of the *New York Sun.*

It happened that I knew about anarchists, because of the execution of the Haymarket martyrs when I was ten years old. In the "chamber of horrors" of the Eden Musee, a place of wax-works, I saw a group representing these desperados sitting round a table making bombs. I swallowed these bombs whole, and shuddered at the thought of depraved persons who inhabited the back rooms of saloons, jeered at God, practiced free love, and conspired to blow up the Government. In short, I believed in 1889 what ninety-five percent of America believes in 1932.

———
———

UPON MY RETURN TO New York in the autumn of 1902, after the writing of *Arthur Stirling,* I met in the office of the *Literary Digest* a tall, soft-voiced, and gentle-souled youth by the name of Leonard D. Abbott; he was a Socialist, so he told me, and he thought I might be interested to know something about that movement. He gave me a couple of pamphlets and a copy of *Wilshire's Magazine.*

It was like the falling down of prison walls about my mind; the most amazing discovery, after all these years—that I did not have to carry the whole burden of humanity's future upon my two frail shoulders! There were actually others who understood; who saw what had gradually become clear to me, that the heart and centre of the evil lay in leaving the social treasure, which nature had created, and which every man has to have in order to live, to become the object of a scramble in the market-place, a delirium of speculation. The principal fact which the Socialists had to teach me was the fact that they themselves existed.

Upton Sinclair's:
A Monthly Magazine
Founding Statement, 1918

"WHEN FINALLY I WAS taken to a public school," Upton Sinclair wrote, I presented the teachers with a peculiar problem; I knew everything but arithmetic. This branch of learning, so essential to a commercial civilization, had shared the fate of alcohol and tobacco, tea and coffee; my mother did not use it so neither did I."[1]

Despite the good intentions of both his mother and the public schools, Sinclair believed his education had given him an inadequate understanding of the economic and political ways of the world. *Upton Sinclair's Magazine* was designed to help provide the kind of education to the public that he believed he had been denied.[2]

By the age of thirteen, Sinclair had enrolled at City College in New York, where "we trooped from one classroom to another and learned by rote what our bored instructors laid out for us."[3] In Ruth Elson's survey of nineteenth-century history texts, she notes that "the schoolbooks are virtually unanimous regarding the evil effect of labor unions."[4] Sinclair would have read descriptions of militant workers as "the idle and vicious," the "dangerous classes," "restless agitators," and "foreigners."

Later, Sinclair attended Columbia University, which also disappointed him. He spent much of his time churning out more than two million words a year of "nickel novels" in order to support his mother and himself. As his books *The Goose Step* and *The Goslings* made clear, Sinclair was deeply dissatisfied with American educational institutions. His most bitter complaint was the lack of accurate, thoughtful political analysis.

Although he considered himself a socialist, Sinclair had supported the American entry into World War I. After the war, he felt bitterly deceived by the tragic waste of young men's lives. His magazine reflects his determination not to be fooled again by his government. He believed that the terms of the Treaty of Versailles would dangerously warp the future of the twentieth century. In 1938, he would set the beginning of his eleven-volume World's End series in 1918, tracing the roots of later social and political inequality and international conflict to that crucial year.

Sinclair's consistent political concern with justice, locally as well as internationally, is confirmed in an interview near the end of his life:

> Any rational man who looks at human society, and sees our enormous, unlimited powers of production at the present time, can find it absolutely inconceivable that we can permit slums to exist and people to live in the degradation and poverty that they do in our great cities.[5]

Notes

1. Upton Sinclair, *The Autobiography of Upton Sinclair* (New York: Harcourt Brace and World) 1962, 21

2. After a year of publishing the magazine, Sinclair negotiated a deal with Kansas publisher Haldeman-Julius, who absorbed the magazine and gave subscribers instead a larger publication, *The New Appeal*, in which Sinclair was guaranteed his own column.

3. Sinclair, *Autobiography*, 23

4. Ruth Miller Elson, *Guardians of Tradition* in Michael Parenti, *History as Mystery* (San Francisco: City Lights, 1999)

5. Ron Gottesman, Interview with Upton Sinclair, Columbia Oral History Project, 1962, 58

THIS IS THE HOUR of a world decision; the greatest crisis which ever has confronted mankind. Upon the course of history during the next few months depends your whole happiness, your whole future. No matter who or what you are, no matter what you wish to do or to be, what you wish your children or your children's children to do or to be—all depends upon this world decision.

And the decision depends upon you. No others can bring you out of peril into safety, no others can give you peace and freedom. You, the people, must know and understand. Hence this magazine— or rather this offer of a magazine; this magazine in embryo, trying to be born.

All the world is suffering from a disease; and it happens that I am an expert on that particular disease. I have lived all my life in a laboratory, where it has been under the microscope; I know the germ, and have the serum ready. So in this world decision I think that I have something to say. So I come with my offer of a magazine.

I have given the would-be publication a name which some will call egotistical. But this is no time for sham modesty. I have a certain trade-mark; I have been twenty years giving a meaning to it, and now I must make use of it. Wherever I have traveled over the world, I have met plenty of prejudice, but I have met no thinking people who did not know my trade-mark, and what it stands for.

It stands for Social Justice. I have preached it in prose and poetry, in magazine articles and strike broadsides and a string of fourteen novels. As Queen Mary said that when she died they would find Calais written on her heart, so on my heart you will find two words, burned in by the acid of pain: Social Justice!

The fundamental cause of this war was that certain youths of the ruling caste of Prussia, living Spartan lives upon a nominal salary, driven by poverty, and with no escape save by marrying the daughters of rich merchants whom they despised, conceived a dream of themselves as pro-consuls, lolling upon silken couches and drinking wine from golden cups in Mesopotamia and the Punjab. Because of this, our boys have to be shipped across the water by thousands and perhaps by millions, and drowned in mud and blood in the trenches of Lorraine.

So I come again with my message of Social Justice. If you really want to do away with the horrors of Armageddon, you have to abolish exploitation, you have to drive poverty from the earth; you have to change the ideas and ideals—not merely of German Junkers, but of American gentlemen, business-men, merchants and masters of affairs. You have to do away with the power of any man, anywhere, to make his comfort and his glory out of the necessities of others; you have to discredit, once and for all time, those pecuniary standards of culture which estimate the excellence of a man by the amount of other people's happiness he can possess and destroy.

My Life and Diet
from *Physical Culture* magazine, 1924

SINCLAIR'S OPENNESS TO medical alternatives was part of his identification with a movement that sought to promote knowledge of health practices among ordinary Americans. During the nineteenth century, medicine was a contested arena as the American Medical Society struggled to outlaw "irregular practices." The Popular Health Movement was a social struggle by feminist and working-class reformers for more effective healthcare.[1] The movement advocated frequent bathing, a healthy diet, and temperance. Although by 1910 many branches of alternative medicine had been outlawed in response to the Flexner Commission report, it continued to enjoy an underground existence.[2] Today, while healthy trends such as bottled water and organic produce are growing,[3] less educated people still lack the kind of information Sinclair saw as especially critical for the working class and unemployed.

Sinclair continued his commitment to health throughout his life. Visitors to Monrovia four years before his death found that he had "limited his diet in the last decade to brown, unhusked rice and fresh fruits three times a day, seven days a week."[4] In his discussion of Sinclair's 1934 campaign for governor, Greg Mitchell comments, "Perhaps there was something to his 'crank' diet after all: Uppie was remarkably fit."[5]

Notes

1. Barbara Ehrenreich and Deirdre English, *Witches, Midwives, and Nurses: A History of Women Healers* (Brooklyn: Feminist Press, 1973)

2. K. Patrick Ober, *Annals of Internal Medicine* 126, January 15, 1997. Ober discusses how the political forces of Jacksonian democracy created an era of unregulated medical practice in the United States.

3. John Robbins, *Diet for a New America* (Walpole, N.H.: Stillpoint Publishing, 1987). See also Frances Moore Lappe, Anna Lappe, *Hope's Edge* (New York: Jeremy Tarcher, 2002).

4. Arthur and Lila Weinberg, "A Saintly Glow," *Washington Post*, October 19, 1964

5. Greg Mitchell, *Campaign of the Century* (New York: Random House, 1992), 576

I T HAS BEEN SAID that no man will ever tell the truth about his own life, because he could not bear the humiliation. But now the proposition is made to me that I shall tell the truth about my search for a diet! I summon my available resolution, and prepare for that strenuous form of spiritual discipline—laughing at one's self.

In order that you may understand this diet extravaganza, let me explain that I am a person with one major vice, the habit of overworking. I am seldom really interested in anything except the writing of a book; and whenever I am bored, I have a way of retiring to a hidden level of consciousness and starting work on the next chapter. I have worked fourteen hours a day for months at a time; and by this means I have supplied myself with a continuous stream of minor ailments.

Most scientists have to provide themselves with a continuous stream of guinea pigs on which to experiment, but I have been my own guinea pig. My purpose might be summed up as an effort to find some diet that would permit me to continue overworking. I may as well say at the outset that I have not found this; but I have learned some other things by the way, and the reader may have the benefit of such expertness as I have acquired in the curing of minor ailments.

Picture me at the age of twenty-one, camping out from April to November upon an island which I share with squirrels and woodpeckers. I am doing my own cooking and am continuously inspired during all my waking hours. Maybe I am not really inspired, of course; but it comes to the same thing, so far as concerns my digestion, which quits after two or three months of such treatment. I visit the local doctor, who tells me that I have dyspepsia, and gives me a pink liquid which contains pepsin, derived from the stomach of a pig. It seems to me a wonderful idea to make a pig do my digesting, so I take a teaspoonful of this liquid after meals, and it works—for two or three weeks.

Then I discover that I need more and more of it, and so gradually I realize that I have not yet solved the health problem.

I drop my writing and turn into a hunter. My hunting, I explain, does not make any great difference in my diet—I am a hunter only for the first fifteen minutes of the hunt—so long as my imagination is intrigued by the idea of being a hunter. Then I forget that I am a hunter and start on the next chapter, and the deer jumps up and is over the brow of the hill before I realize why I am carrying a gun. The same thing happens when my fellow hunters put me on a "stand" to watch for a deer; I forget where I am, and what I am there for, and the deer comes up and sniffs the back of my neck before I hear him.

But hunting takes me outdoors, and makes me walk long distances, and so for years it remains the solution of my health problem—alternatively overworking and taking hunting trips. Then I make the same discovery as in the case of the pig pepsin. My periods of work grow shorter and shorter, and my periods of hunting grow longer and longer.

I am forced to the idea that I must be eating the wrong things; and so begin my diet experiments.

Four or five years have passed, and my inspiration, real or imagined, plus my fourteen hours per day of work, have brought me notoriety and a large sum of money; also they have brought me close to the verge of nervous collapse. My hair is falling out in showers, my teeth are developing abscesses, I am plagued with headaches and insomnia, and I catch a cold if I poke my head outdoors without a hat on it. The cold will last for two or three months, and I go to the doctors and have my nose pumped full of pink and green and yellow and black and purple liquids, which do me not the slightest good. I go to a hair specialist to be told what to do for my hair, and I do it religiously, with no results. I go to the teeth specialists and have one tooth treated, only to have another one go wrong.

I may as well close this painful portion of my story by saying that I have patronized every kind of orthodox medical man there is, I have paid out a great many thousands of hard-earned dollars, and with the exception of a necessary surgical operation, I cannot discover that I have ever obtained one particle of benefit, not even any information—except the single bit of information that the doctors do not understand the causes or the cure of disease.

I had now got to the stage of physical and financial progress where a man begins to visit sanitariums. Of course, I did not know what sanitarium to visit, so I picked out the one which was most advertised. It happened to be a vegetarian institution, and I went there and was converted to the religion of vegetarianism, and lived on the patented vegetarian foods which this institution sells; I had myself pounded and rubbed and baked and boiled and frozen and shaken and analyzed and measured and weighed and microscoped and telescoped and electrocuted, and I know not what else.

I can sum up the story of this sanitarium in a paragraph. Their foods are utter rubbish from first to last, and their sole effective method of treatment consists of stimulating the intestinal functions by means of heat and cold and massage. This has the effect of relieving constipation, and so long as you take the treatment your health is benefited. The moment you stop, your health is just where it was before; and if you were to go on with the treatment indefinitely, you would find it just like the pig pepsin, you would need more and more of it—you may see that proven upon the old-timers, who spend all their lives being "treated" in one way or another.

A little before this, I had discovered Horace Fletcher, and therefore I was diligently chewing to a paste all these various mushy and tasteless vegetable foods. I was plagued with incessant headaches, and when I left the sanitarium they became so bad that I went off in desperation by myself, and for six months did no brain work, and lived outdoors, trying a wonderful new diet wrinkle which I had heard about—the raw food diet, or, as my friends derisively called it, the "squirrel diet."

I never followed it quite strictly; I used every day a little of some cooked whole-wheat product, like shredded wheat biscuit or graham crackers. Apart from this I lived on nuts, raw salads, ripe olives, and fresh fruits. It was the first time since I had taken to writing books that I lived for six months without an ache or a pain. It was a marvelous experience, and so I became a sworn devotee of the squirrel diet—entirely overlooking the real cause of the phenomenon, that I had quit doing hard brain work. I was riding horses, playing tennis, swimming, walking, and reading other people's books. After six months of this I thought I had solved my problem, and plunged into the writing of another book—only to find in the course of a few months that I was right back where I was before.

I believe that the raw food diet as I have outlined it above is the ideal diet for an athlete, or for a person doing physical labor. But when you come to do hard brain work, such as I do, involving intense concentration and continual nervous strain, you simply have not the nervous energy to digest raw foods. And then a most terrible thing happens; I won't go into details, but will simply cite the phrase which I invented—I used to say I had a balloon inside me. The ordinary balloons of commerce, I believe, are filled with hydrogen gas, while the product of fermentation of bananas and soaked prunes is carbon dioxide. So I did not go up into the air, I just stayed on the earth, and sat around in corners, and looked miserable, and moaned. I did this for two or three years, keeping at the diet most stubbornly and religiously, being lured on by the memory of those six months of perfect health.

Through the clouds of my misery there broke a new dawn: Bernarr Macfadden told me about fasting, and I proceeded to try that. I presume that in an article on diet it is proper to deal with the negation of diet so I tell briefly about fasting. It is a discovery which we human beings have to make all over again—having forgotten it when we ceased to be animal. When a cat or dog is sick it stops eating; only human beings let the doctors go on feeding them with death in the form of "slops." (That is a painful phrase, but it is the doctor's, not mine.)

The fast is a real thing, and one of my discoveries which I have kept. It is, I believe, a natural process, whereby the body shuts down its digestive and assimilative functions, and lives upon its own surplus tissue, while it cleans house of almost all diseases. You can fast for thirty or forty days without harm, but this involves a nervous strain, and I do not advocate it except under experienced guidance. A fast of ten or twelve days, with nothing whatever except water, will not hurt anyone, old or young, rich or poor. I have taken several such, and have received letters from many hundreds of people who have done the same, with almost uniform benefits.

I took this first fast in Bernarr Macfadden's sanitarium, and after it, at his suggestion, I took a milk diet for two or three weeks. Here is another wonderful discovery. You drink a glass of milk every twenty minutes, and you lie bathed in delightful contentment, and gain one or two pounds a day, and go forth to a new life. This first milk diet of mine was a success; afterward I tried it many times, and it always failed. Why this happened is one of the mysteries of my life. Some day, doubtless, science will find out all about this milk diet, and how it works, both in success and failure. All I can say is that when it goes, it is like floating down a beautiful stream in a canoe, and when it doesn't go, it is like a trip through Dante's "Inferno." I am sure no respectable magazine editor could publish a description of the consequences of having ten or twenty quarts of milk turn sour inside a human body!

From my first fast and milk diet I went away rejuvenated—but only to renew the painful discovery that I was not yet free to over-work. Matters were complicated by the fact that I had gone back to that wonderful raw food diet, and was once more a victim of carbon dioxide generated from undigested bananas and soaked prunes. But now somebody came along and took pity on my misery, and gave me a book by the late Dr. Salisbury, inventor of the so-called "meat diet." Most people believe that this requires eating raw meat, but that is a slander; it is just ordinary hamburg steaks, but made without fat or gristle. There is no carbon in a hamburg steak, so you cannot make carbon dioxide out of it. Dr. Salisbury has a phrase by which he described the effects of the ordinary diet of human beings—he called it "making a yeast-pot of your stomach," and this phrase struck a sympathetic echo in my soul.

I had been a religious vegetarian for at least three years; and now I was confronted with the problem of getting a hamburg steak. I remember walking up and down in front of a butcher store for an hour or so, trying to get up the courage to go in. You might reproduce my emotions if you would picture yourself on the point of entering a morgue and ordering a slice of baby cutlet! However, I finally got up the courage, and I made the discovery that the butcher would sell me a piece of beefsteak without asking any questions whatever, or expressing any horror at my backsliding. I went home and had my first beefsteak in many years, and have never been a vegetarian since.

The newspaper reporters had had much fun with my squirrel diet, and the late Eugene Wood now wrote an article about me, in which he referred to me as "the celebrated advocate of raw food who is now living upon a diet of stewed beefsteak." As a matter of fact, it wasn't quite as bad as that; it was simply that I was doing my cooking over a tiny oil stove, and couldn't do anything to the beefsteaks but let them stew! I remember Jack London's remarking that the only man who could really cook a beefsteak properly was a locomotive fireman, because he had a hot fire and a clean shovel. That came later, and I now know how to cook my meat. But at that time I ate it soft and soggy; anyhow, it did not ferment, and I made the discovery that for a man doing hard brain work, lean beef is the most perfectly assimilated of all foods.

Let me add this, for the comfort of my vegetarian friends. I recognize that meat-eating is a habit both costly and dirty. Of course, we put the dirty work off on other people; nevertheless, it makes a dirty world. I am quite sure that in the course of time science will discover the laws of diet, and enable us to maintain health without slaughtering our fellow creatures. I know that children can be brought up on a vegetarian diet, I know that athletes can achieve records on it. I know also that nobody ought to work as hard as I do and in a happy world, from which war and oppression have been banished, all men and women may be serene and take time for play. But meantime, I want to write some books which I think are needed, and I take the liberty of causing the death of a few cows and sheep and pigs in order to make this writing possible.

This was the last of my dietetic crusades—unless you want to count such details as swallowing several tablespoonfuls of sand every day as a remedy for constipation. I think I have tried every kind of dietetic extravagance I ever heard of, except just one—I have never been able to get up the nerve for the so-called "dry diet," in which you eat unlimited quantities of white bread and other starchy products without any water! Incredible as it may seem, there are people who insist they have got well that way. All I can say is, I have been the world's dietetic guinea pig long enough, and am leaving further discoveries to posterity.

You will want to get something serious out of my misadventures, so I will explain that I got a little something out of nearly all my experiments; the regimen of health upon which I live is a combination of them all. I have cut out the obvious eccentricities, and dropped all hard and fast rules. I can find something to eat on anybody's table, and I am careful to nibble a little of everything, because I know the hostess is watching me with an eagle eye; she has heard that I am some kind of a diet crank, and has been worrying about what she ought to provide for me; also she is looking for a chance to talk about the subject which bores me more than any other subject in the world!

You know how it is at dinner-parties nowadays; everybody talks about Prohibition, and you can't get any other subject in edgeways. When I come along, everybody starts to talk about diet. Before I get the first morsel into my mouth, someone says: "Why, I thought you believed in fasting!" When the soup comes, they tactfully inform me that there is no meat in it. Before I have swallowed the first oyster, the discussion of vegetarianism is in full swing.

However, being a home-body, it doesn't matter so much to me; I can follow my own desires most of the time. We do not keep a servant in our home, so our first rule is extreme simplicity, with the exclusion of everything which cannot be prepared in a few minutes. Most people are used to having someone spend hours preparing their food, so they shudder at the very sound of my diet.

This morning for my breakfast I had a slice of whole wheat bread, a stewed apple, a ripe banana, and a few raisins. When I finish this article I shall have a good-sized chunk of beefsteak, which I shall cook myself, because nobody else in the family has ever learned to cook it quickly and keep the juices in it; some lettuce or celery, which can be washed in a hurry, and perhaps a potato which was boiled during the last meal and warmed up quickly; and finally, a little fruit.

My supper will be the same as breakfast, except that there will be some other kind of fruit.

I restrict my diet in the following ways. I am careful not to have an excess of starch; and except when I am out in company, I seldom eat any white flour product. I also avoid excessive fat; I do not eat the fat of meat, but get along with a little butter, and occasionally some ripe olives, in addition to such fat as one gets in eating lean meat. Also I regard the ordinary refined sugar as a form of slow poison. I eat a little of it when I come upon it in a dessert, but when I am at home I get my sugar in the form of figs, raisins, dates, and prunes.

One of the most important of all physiological truths is this: the mineral salts which come in natural foods are necessary to the body, and one of the leading causes of disease is the eating of prepared foods from which these salts have been removed. When the foods are burned up in the cells of your body, a great number of chemical poisons are produced. These poisons have to be removed from the body, and this means a complicated set of chemical processes; if any of the salts are missing from the diet, these processes cannot take place, and your body is poisoned instead of nourished. Just how much you need of these various salts nobody can say at present; the only safe rule is to eat foods in their natural state. Equally important is the supply of vitamines, and you will notice that the foods I prescribe are those which are rich in vitamines.

The next most important rule is not to overeat; perhaps I might call that the first of all rules. In fact, I would go so far as to say that a small quantity of a bad diet is better for you than an excess of the best diet. There may be a few highly strung and nervous individuals who do not eat enough, but as a general rule human beings eat thirty or forty per cent more than they ought to eat. The life insurance statistics reveal that people who are ten pounds under the normal weight for their height have approximately five per cent additional life expectancy, while people who are ten pounds over the normal have approximately five per cent less of life expectancy. That ought to settle the question of whether to eat more or less. You have nothing to worry about in eating less, because nature will take care of it; you will not be permitted to fade away without realizing it.

So it is a safe rule to get along with as little food as will suffice you without discomfort. Another safe rule is that as you get older you should eat less.

We in our family have the habit of going every now and then upon what we call "crusades"; that is to say, we come upon some social wrong more cruel than we can endure to know about, and we start a publicity campaign, which sometimes includes the adventure of going to jail. In any case, we are wrought up to a considerable emotional pitch, and we give many newspaper interviews, and write many articles and letters and miscellaneous propaganda. Manifestly, under such conditions we cannot digest the normal amount of food; we have noticed that we lose all interest in food, and we do not let that worry us. During two or three months of the Colorado coal strike, and our so-called "mourning pickets," my diet would consist of a couple of meals a day, such as a baked apple and some graham crackers, or perhaps a dish of ice cream. At the end of the ordeal there would be ten or twenty pounds less of me, but I have found that does no harm whatever, if you are careful not to try to make up that lost weight all at once. It is the same thing as in the case of fasting; your appetite will come back with a rush, and you will have to let yourself stay hungry, and make up your loss by slow stages.

Another very essential rule: no human being can be well who does not exercise, sufficiently to perspire vigorously for an hour at least three times a week. There was a rule in the armies of King Cyrus, that every man had to sweat once every day. Nature will take care of that when you are young, if you are outdoors and have room enough to play in; but the modern business man shuts himself up in a stuffy office and sits all day at a desk, when it would be better for him if he were downstairs with his coat off, helping to load one of the trucks. The best thing he can think of is to go out and knock a little white ball around a field—which I suppose is all right, if a man can bring himself to stand it intellectually.

The last rule of all is not to worry about your diet. I have broken that rule many times myself, and it is only of late years that I have come to realize the importance of it. I have seen my wife, an intense and highly strung woman, worry herself into a bad case of varicose veins, and then cure them completely in a few weeks by the method of auto-suggestion taught by Coué. I have no doubt that a great proportion of people worry themselves into stomach and intestinal troubles. So I say, get yourself a simple and rational diet, consisting of the natural and wholesome foods upon which our race has been developed, and get plenty of fresh air and exercise, and a reasonable amount of sleep, and then learn as quickly as possible to forget your diet, and all the rest of your physical problems, and interest yourself in something worthwhile in life—somebody or some cause outside of yourself. That is the great secret of health, both of mind and body, as well as of all happiness and true success in life.

Two

"The Land of Orange Groves and Jails": Impressions of California

The main industry of Southern California is its climate, its social life is display, its intellectual life is "boosting," and its politics are run by chambers of commerce and real estate exchanges.
— Upton Sinclair, The Brass Check, 1920

IN 1908, SINCLAIR VISITED poet George Sterling in Carmel, where he hoped to set up "an outdoor Helicon Hall beside the Pacific."[1] Although he was never able to replicate that utopian colony, in 1915 he and his wife decided to move to California. They bought a rose-covered home on Sunset Avenue in Pasadena near the Arroyo Seco, where they lived until 1940. Visitors to Pasadena included Gertrude Atherton, King Gillette (founder of the razor fortune, whom Sinclair would successfully convert to socialism), Bertrand Russell, and Albert Einstein.

Once he had settled in Southern California, Sinclair rarely left.[2] In an interview, he remarked:

Since moving here in 1915, I've never been able to live anywhere else. Friends ask me, "how can you stand"—the reactionary politics, and the anti-union atmosphere—and my answer is that people are much the same the world over, but here the climate makes it possible to be so much more active.[3]

From his vantage point in Pasadena, Sinclair quickly found evidence of corruption, particularly between industry and the press.

In Pasadena, Sinclair played doubles tennis every Sunday morning with prominent businessmen; by 1926, he was rated eighth among the top tennis players in town.

He began a series of magazine articles and books detailing what he had uncovered. His efforts to expose the *Los Angeles Times*, recounted in *The Brass Check* and *The Goslings*, were widely read. In retaliation, the *Times* initiated an attack on Sinclair, describing him as "an effeminate young man with a fatuous smile, a weak chin and a sloping forehead, talking in a false treble."[4] This distorted characterization contradicted by anyone who knew him personally would nonetheless influence historians long after Sinclair's death.

The local Pasadena paper was more accepting; it characterized him as "mild-mannered and living the simple life."[5] Sinclair, who had joined the local chapter of the Socialist Party and had become its chair, also played doubles tennis every Sunday morning with prominent businessmen and the Valley Hunt Club. The results of his victories in local tournaments were duly reported, and in 1926 he was rated eighth among the top tennis players in Pasadena.[6]

Although many writers were sympathetic to the struggles of organized labor in California, few took physical risks or otherwise put themselves in harm's way to arouse public indignation over the treatment of workers.[7] Forty years after the events at Liberty Hill, a brutal confrontation between a hired mob and striking IWW dock workers that resulted in the arrest of Sinclair and many others, Mario Savio would urge: "You've got to put your bodies upon the wheels, upon the levers."[8] How ironic it is that Upton Sinclair, ridiculed for his alleged sissiness, was one of the very few writers who dared to do exactly that.

The story of what happened to the striking Wobblies in San Pedro is part of the forgotten history of California; historian John Gager has noted that the voices of the powerless, when heard at all, are "transmitted through a carefully tuned network of filters."[9] But as sociologist James Loewen has argued, despite the miseducation they may have endured, Americans relish learning the untold stories of the past.[10] The story of Liberty Hill is largely untold, and so is the story of the impact of oil in California. Sinclair's wife, Mary Craig, owned property in Signal Hill (near Long Beach), site of a Shell Oil "wildcat" well that had spouted a 114-foot black geyser, proclaiming the birth of one of the world's greatest oil fields. About the story that became Sinclair's novel *Oil!*, Craig recalled:

> "Are you going to write about it?" I asked.
>
> "Gosh!" came the response. "Don't you see what we've got here? Human nature lay bare! Competition in *excelsis*. The whole industry—free, gratis, for nothing! How could I pass it up!"[11]

Another rarely told story is that of Yetta Stromberg and her co-defendants, who were convicted of running a summer camp in Yucaipa, California. Sinclair wrote an article about their arrest and trial for "The Open Forum," the newsletter of Southern California's American Civil Liberties Union. He titled it aptly with the Wobblies' description of Southern California: "Land of Orange Groves and Jails."

Notes

1. Helicon Hall was Sinclair's 1907 effort to set up a cooperative colony in New Jersey where it was hoped that "answers would evolve to some of the hotly debated questions of the day concerning child care, diet, and the right of women to participate in making decisions." (Jon Yoder, *Upton Sinclair*, New York: Ungar Publishing, 1975, 49). See also Peggy Ann Brown, "Not Your Usual Boardinghouse

Types: Upton Sinclair's Helicon Home Colony 1906–7" (Ph.D. dissertation, American University, 1993).

2. Yet in a recent series on American writers on C-Span, the section on Upton Sinclair was set in a Chicago slaughterhouse of today and entirely omitted his California life.

3. Judson Grenier, "Upton Sinclair: The Road to California," *Southern California Quarterly* LVI:4, Winter 1974, 325 (based on a 1916 interview)

4. *Los Angeles Times*, June 25, 1916

5. Grenier, "Road to California," 331

6. Sinclair explained, "Tennis playing became a religion with me...one of my opponents here in Pasadena called me 'the human rabbit.'...I played tennis with the utmost delight." (Ron Gottesman, Interview with Upton Sinclair, Columbia Oral History Project, 99)

7. When Sinclair was interviewed at the age of 86, he said, "I have given the [auto workers' union] this house after both my wife and I die. They are to put up a fund and award a prize for the best literary work in the cause of of labor and social justice." (Arthur and Lila Weinberg, "A Saintly Glow," *Washington Post*, October 18, 1964) The house he was referring to in Monrovia is now in private ownership and there is no existing Upton Sinclair House.

8. Mario Savio, December 3, 1964, quoted in D. L. Goines, *The Free Speech Movement: Coming of Age in the 1960's* (Berkeley: Ten Speed, 1993), 122

9. John Gager, from *The Origins of Anti-Semitism: Attitudes Toward Judaism in Pagan and Christian Antiquity*, in Michael Parenti, *History as Mystery* (San Francisco: City Lights, 1999), 16

10. James Loewen, *Lies My Teachers Told Me* (New York: Simon and Schuster, 1995)

11. Mary Craig Sinclair, *Southern Belle* (New York: Crown Publishers, 1957), 280

Wandering
from *American Outpost: A Book of Reminiscences*, 1932

IN HIS AUTOBIOGRAPHY, Sinclair recalled:

My friend Gaylord Wilshire now had a gold mine, high up in the eastern slope of the Sierra mountains; also George Sterling, the poet, was begging me to come to Carmel and visit him; so I set out over the pathway of the Argonauts in a Pullman car.[1]

Gaylord Wilshire (for whom Wilshire Boulevard in Los Angeles is named) had become a confirmed socialist and was now publishing his own magazine. As Sinclair described him:

> He wore a little pointed black beard and moustache. He had a very quiet manner and a delightful, dry sense of humor...When I first met him, I saw right away that he was a remarkable man and I began sending him articles.[2]

Wilshire was trying to create a socialist experiment in mining; it was run "on a basis of comradeship, with high wages and plenty of socialist propaganda," Sinclair reported.[3] But it failed to produce gold with enough commercial qualities, and its residents lost their savings.

Sinclair took Gaylord and Mary Wilshire on his visit to Carmel. Carmel was the center of an informal community of writers and artists that had its decade of greatest vitality between 1904 and 1914. George Sterling had settled there first, "remaining for ten years as symbolic founder, master of the revels, and a guru-in-chief."[4] Although today George Sterling's work may seem overly sentimental, Sinclair valued him deeply as a friend and a poet.[5] Lincoln Steffens had already visited, and Mary Austin was in residence, writing about the problems of the intellectual woman in *Santa Lucia*. During his visit, Sinclair wrote three one-act plays, one of which featured John D. Rockefeller debating "the author" on a Carmel beach.[6]

In his essay "Upton Sinclair in Carmel," Franklin Walker comments derisively, "The principle phase of his activity which left its trace on Carmel lore was his diet...while others ate mussels and abalones and mountain venison, he munched on big, red, luscious tomatoes."[7] Together with another Carmel resident, Michael Williams, Sinclair wrote *Good Health and How We Won It*, published the year after this visit.[8]

Notes:

1. Upton Sinclair, *The Autobiography of Upton Sinclair* (New York: Harcourt Brace and World, 1962), 146

2. Ron Gottesman, Interview with Upton Sinclair, Columbia Oral History Project, 77-78

3. Upton Sinclair, *American Outpost* (New York: Farrar and Rinehart Inc., 1932), 208-209

4. Kevin Starr, *Americans and the California Dream* (New York: Oxford University Press, 1973), 267

5. In 1936, in a talk for the Western Writers Conference at the Scottish Rite Auditorium in San Francisco, Sinclair described George Sterling as his dearest friend ("Four California Friends: A Talk by Upton Sinclair," *EPIC News*, December 7, 1936).

6. Upton Sinclair, *Plays of Protest* (New York: Mitchell and Kennerley, 1912)

7. Franklin Walker, *The Seacoast of Bohemia* (Los Angeles: Book Club of California, 1966), quoted in *Upton Sinclair Quarterly* IV:2, June 1980, 4-5

8. Upton Sinclair, *Good Health and How We Won It* (New York: Frederick Stokes Company, 1909). Michael Williams was an ex-resident of Helicon.

A DAY'S JOURNEY on the little railroad which runs in back of the Sierras, through the red deserts of Nevada. In the little town of Bishop, California, the Wilshires met me, and we rode saddle-horses up to the mine, eighteen miles in the mountains. A high valley with Bishop Creek running through, and towering peaks all about, and cold, clear lakes—the first snows of the year were falling, and trout had quit biting, but I climbed the peaks, and ate large meals in the dining-room with the miners. The camp was run on a basis of comradeship, with high wages and plenty of Socialist propaganda; we slept in a rough shack, and in the evenings discussed the mine with the superintendent and foreman and assayer. These were old-time mining-men, and were of one accord that here was the greatest gold-mine in America. You could see the vein, all the way up the mountainside, and down in the workings you could knock pieces off the face and bring them up and have them assayed before your eyes.

But alas, there were complications in quartz-mining beyond my understanding. Most of the vein was low-grade, and could only be made to pay upon a large scale. Wilshire did not have the capital to work it in that way, and in the effort to get the money he bled himself, and thousands of readers of his magazine who had been brought to share his rosy hopes. I stood by him through that long ordeal, and know that he did everything—except to turn the mine

Sinclair home in Pasadena, 1916–1926
Sinclair explained in his autobiography: "We had decided we wanted to get away from ocean winds; and I had met a tennis professional who lived in Pasadena and who assured me I would find plenty of tennis there…It was an especially good home for us because Craig could have her room at the south end and I could practice my violin at the north end."

Long Beach, 1926–1930
Mary Craig remembered, in her autobiography, *Southern Belle:* "I could step out my front door in a bathing suit with no house between me and the ocean. On the other side, and separated only by a narrow strip of sand, was placid Alamitos Bay."

Beverly Hills, 1931–1941
Sinclair recalled in *I, Candidate for Governor: And How I Got Licked* that
he "found myself tied up with [the film] *Thunder over Mexico,* and having
to go over to Hollywood nearly every day; then, as we had no money to finish
the picture, I had to work for one of the studios, which meant going to Culver
City every day through traffic. I found it wearing, and went over to Hollywood
to find a house to rent."

Monrovia, 1942–1966
The Sinclairs moved to Monrovia in 1942, from where, Upton wrote, "we can
see the Pacific Ocean, some 20 or 30 miles away. That is, we could see it
when the air was clear, but since the war began Los Angeles has become an
industrial district, as smoky as London.

over to some of the big capitalist groups which sought to buy it and freeze out the old stockholders.

Socialists ought not to fool with money-making schemes in capitalist society. I have heard that said a hundred times, and I guess it is right; but there is something to be noted on the other side. The Socialists of America have never been able to maintain an organ of propaganda upon a national scale; the country is too big, and the amount of capital required is beyond their resources. The *Appeal to Reason* was a gift to them from a real estate speculator with a conscience, old J. A. Wayland—may the managers of the next world be pitiful to him. (His Catholic enemies set a trap for him, baited with a woman; he crossed a state line in her company, which is a prison offense in our pious America, and when he got caught, he blew out his brains.) *Wilshire's Magazine* was a gift from a billboard advertising man with a sense of humor. So long as his money lasted, we took his gift with thanks; if his gold-mining gamble had succeeded, we would all have made money, and had a still bigger magazine, and everything would have been lovely. My old friend "Gay" died recently in a hospital in New York, all crippled up with arthritis. I miss his fertile mind, and his sly, quiet smile.

ON TO CARMEL, a town which boasts more scenery to the square mile than any other place I know; a broad beach, bordered by deep pine woods, and flanked by rocky headlands; at one side a valley, with farms, and a river running through it, and mountains beyond. Twenty years ago the place was owned by a real estate speculator of the Bohemian Club type; that is to say, a person with an art-bug in his head, who would donate a lot to any celebrity who would confer the honor of his presence. Needless to say, George Sterling, the Bohemian Club's poet laureate, had his pick of lots, and a bungalow on a little knoll by the edge of a wood, remote from traffic and "boosting."

George was at this time forty, but showing no signs of age. He was tall and spare, built like an Indian, with a face whose resemblance to Dante has often been noted. When he was with the roistering San Francisco crew he drank, but when he was alone he lived the life of an athlete in training; he cut wood, hunted, walked miles in the mountains, and swam miles in the sea. A charming companion, tender-hearted as a child, bitter only against cruelty and greed; incidentally a fastidious poet, aloof and dedicated.

His friend Arnold Genthe gave me the use of a cottage, and there I lived alone for two or three months of winter, in peace and happiness unknown to me hitherto. I had been reading literature of the health cranks, and had resolved upon a drastic experiment; I would try the raw food diet, for which so much was promised. I ate two meals a day, of nuts, fruits, olives, and salad vegetables; the only cooked food being two or three shredded wheat biscuit or some graham crackers. The diet agreed with me marvelously, and for the entire period I never had an ache or pain. So I was triumphant; entirely overlooking the fact that I was doing none of the nerve-destroying labor of creative writing. I was reading, walking, riding horseback, playing tennis, meeting with George and other friends; if I had done that all my life I might never have had an ache or pain.

In Oakland was the Ruskin Club, an organization of Socialist intellectuals, who wanted to give a dinner and hear me make a speech. George and I went up to town, and George stopped in the Bohemian Club, and stood in front of the bar with his boon companions, and I stood with him and drank a glass of orange juice, as is my custom. Then we set out for the ferry, George talking rapidly, and I listening, in a strange state of uncertainty. I couldn't understand what George was saying, and I couldn't understand why. It wasn't until we got to Oakland that I realized what was the matter; my California Dante was drunk. When we got to the dinner, someone who knew him better than I took him off and walked him around the block and fed him bromo-seltzers; the Socialist poem which he had written for the occasion had to be read by someone else.

I went back to Carmel alone, feeling most sorrowful. I was used to my poor old father getting drunk, and some of my other men relatives, but this was the first time I had ever seen a great mind distorted by alcohol. I wrote George a note, telling him that I was leaving Carmel, because I could not be happy there. George came running over to my place at once, and with tears in his eyes pleaded forgiveness. He swore that he had had only two drinks; it was because he had taken them on an empty stomach. But I knew that sort of drinker's talk, and it did not move me. Then he swore that if I would stay, he would not touch another drop while I was in California. That promise I accepted, and he kept it religiously. Many a time I have thought my best service to letters would have been to stay right there the rest of my days!

Singing Jailbirds
Postscript and Act I, Scene I,
and Upton Sinclair's letter to the Los Angeles
chief of police from *The Nation*, 1923–1924

> I found it impossible to keep my peace of mind in a "bull pen" civilization, and decided to do what I could to remind the authorities of Southern California that there is still supposed to be a Constitution in the country.
> —*Upton Sinclair*, The Goslings, 1924

HISTORIAN MIKE DAVIS tells us that the culminating battle in what he calls the "Forty-Year War for the Open Shop" was the defeat of militant longshoremen, sailors, and oil workers in the Los Angeles harbor from 1921 to 1923.[1] After the IWW revolt of dock workers erupted there at "Liberty Hill," Mary Craig Sinclair described a visit from a woman who "vividly described atrocities when a hired mob raided a meeting, beating workers, throwing a little girl into a receptacle of boiling coffee, scalding her almost to death."[2] Martin Zanger argues that Sinclair's advocacy for the dock workers may have stimulated his willingness to run a campaign for governor, noting that "subsequent California history might well have evolved differently had Mary Craig held her husband to his promise to stay out of the Wobbly strike."[3]

The year following his arrest, Sinclair wrote *Singing Jailbirds*, set in "the harbor jail in a California city," to draw attention to the treatment of jailed Wobblies. During the First World War, many antiwar activists were jailed at the direction of Attorney General A. Mitchell Palmer, who had launched an unconstitutional series of nationwide attacks on radical and socialist groups around the country. Among the jailed activists was Ralph Chaplin, author of the union anthem "Solidarity Forever." From Leavenworth, Chaplin wrote, "It was letters from the outside world that helped me most to keep courage."[4] After Chaplin was released, he visited George Sterling in San Francisco and discovered that Sterling's interest in his cause, and in the cause of all jailed Wobblies—members of the International Workers of the World (IWW)—had been influenced by Upton Sinclair.

Following successful performances in Berlin in 1927, *Singing Jailbirds* ran for two months (1928–1929) at the New Playwrights Theater in New York to favorable reviews. The *New York Daily News* said, "The element of truth always to be found in Sinclair's writings is evident in this grim tragedy of the labor class."

German scholar Dieter Herms notes indignantly that Sinclair criticism has "outrageously ignored Sinclair the playwright."[5] Herms argues that Sinclair's play represents the beginnings of agit-prop drama in America in the early twentieth century (when Herms discovered the San Francisco Mime Troupe doing a very similar kind of radical agit-prop in 1978, he brought them to Germany to perform).[6]

Immediately after the battle at Liberty Hill, Sinclair joined friends in Los Angeles to organize the Southern California chapter of the American Civil Liberties Union. In 1983, the Southern California ACLU celebrated its sixtieth anniversary with an outdoor reception. They had announced excerpts from *Singing Jailbirds* as the centerpiece of the program, but "when the time came, master of ceremonies Ned Beatty announced that Sinclair's words were 'too angry, too bitter' to be part of a lawn party on a beautiful afternoon."[7]

The battle for Liberty Hill was finally given historical recognition in 1998, after twenty years of effort by retired longshoreman Art Almeida. In 1952, Almeida met an old IWW member, who sold him a biography of Joe Hill; he developed "an insatiable appetite to know more."[8] Although the original waterfront bluffs have been leveled, Almeida found a stonemason to create a monument of rock and shells, now installed in front of the Los Angeles harbor workers' community center. It reads:

> In 1923 the Marine Transport Workers Industrial Union 510, a branch of the Industrial Workers of the World (IWW), called a strike that immobilized 90 ships here in San Pedro. The union protested low wages, bad working conditions, and the imprisonment of union activists under California's criminal syndicalism law. Denied access to public property, strikers and their supporters rallied here at this site they called "Liberty Hill." Writer Upton Sinclair was arrested for reading from the Bill of Rights to a large gathering. The strike failed but laid a foundation for success in the 1930s. The syndicalism law was ruled unconstitutional in 1968.

Notes:

1. Mike Davis, "Sunshine and the Open Shop" in *Metropolis in the Making: Los Angeles in the 1920's*, ed. Tom Sitton and William Deverell (University of California Press, Berkeley, 2001), 102

2. Mary Craig Sinclair, *Southern Belle* (New York, Crown Publishers, 1957) 280

3. Martin Zanger, "The Reluctant Activist: Upton Sinclair's Reform Activities in California 1915–1930" (Ph.D. dissertation, University of Michigan, 1971), 406

4. Ralph Chaplin, *Wobbly: The Rough and Tumble Story of an American Radical* (Chicago: University of Chicago, 1948), 254

5. Dieter Herms, "The Novelist and Dramatist: A Note on Upton Sinclair's Plays" in *Upton Sinclair Quarterly* VII, Summer/Fall 1983, 2–3. Herms focuses his essay on his favorites from the twenty-nine published scripts, including *John D, Oil!* and *Singing Jailbirds*.

6. According to Mime Troupe member Bruce Bawer, Herms personally guaranteed audiences and brought the troupe to an enthusiastic German public four times during the 1980s. For more on the Mime Troupe, see www.sfmt.org.

7. John Ahouse, "ACLU Honor Founder Sinclair," *Upton Sinclair Quarterly* 7:1, Spring 1983, 3. Ahouse adds, "It was indeed a lovely afternoon, on which 'down in the salt mines' labor problems would have seemed very far away" (personal correspondence, Ahouse to Coodley, December 13, 1996).

8. Lauren Coodley, Oral History of Art Almeida, in "Liberty Hill Becomes a State Historic Landmark," *The Dispatcher*, March 1998. Almeida published "Liberty Hill Shone as San Pedro Labor Beacon" in *California Historian* 44:3, Spring 1998.

F OR THE BENEFIT of those readers who ask to what extent conditions pictured in this play really exist:

The impulse to write the play came as a result of an experience in the strike of the Marine Transport Workers at San Pedro, California, the harbor of Los Angeles, in May 1923. The writer was arrested with three friends and held in jail "incommunicado" for eighteen hours, for the offense of having attempted to read the Constitution of the United States, while standing on private property in San Pedro, with the written permission of the owner, and after due notice to the mayor of the city and to the police authorities. Those who care to know about this strike and the conditions leading up to it will find an account in the opening chapters of *The Goslings*. In the *Nation*, for June 6, 1923, they will find the writer's letter to the chief of police of Los Angeles, who did the arresting.

In this strike six hundred men were jailed in one night, for the offense of manifesting by cheering and singing their sympathy with the strike. Scene II of Act I, portraying conditions in the "tanks," is an exact account of what happened in the police station at San Pedro, and in the various city jails of Los Angeles. The "Dominie" in the play is the Reverend George Chalmers Richmond, formerly rector of Old St. John's Episcopal Church, Philadelphia; Dr. Richmond was arrested under the conditions described, and behaved in the jail as described. Subsequently the various abuses of prisoners and violations of law by the police were investigated by a committee of the Ministers' Association of Los Angeles. Before this committee, and in the presence of the writer, Police Captain Plummer, in charge at San Pedro, stated: "I broke that strike." Before this same committee one member of the IWW testified how he had been personally struck in the face again and again, and otherwise beaten, by the then chief of police of Los Angeles, and several other men testified to having witnessed this and other brutalities. The police authorities admitted in a formal report that they had stopped the singing of the prisoners by shutting off all ventilation in the tanks. They denied having turned on the steam heat, as a large number of the prisoners asserted had been done.

It is only fair to the police authorities of Los Angeles to state that exactly similar things have been done and exactly similar conditions prevail in jails and prisons throughout the United States. If anyone feels doubt on this question, he is advised to read *In Prison*, by Kate Richards O'Hare, a woman who served several years in a federal prison for the crime of having expressed an unpopular political conviction. The reader is also advised to familiarize himself with a book entitled *Crucibles of Crime*, by Joseph F. Fishman, who as prison inspector for the United States government made over sixteen thousand visits of inspection to prisons and jails throughout the United States. When the reader has finished these two books he will have less doubt about incidents in this play.

In order to avoid misunderstanding, the writer wishes to state that he does not belong to the IWW, and never has belonged to it; as a Socialist, he disapproves of the IWW program, and has never hesitated to make that disapproval known. But he stands for the right of all groups of men and women to voice their political and social opinions; and his play is an appeal to the American people to re-establish the most fundamental of constitutional rights, free speech, free press, and free assemblage.

At the time this play is completed, May 1924, there are in the prisons of the United States 114 men and women whose only offense—the only offense charged—has been the holding and advocating of certain political ideas. Four or five years ago there were between 1,000 and 1,500 such prisoners. In the State of

After his 1923 arrest for reading the Bill of Rights to striking longshoremen, Sinclair publicized the episode as a means of launching the Southern California branch of the American Civil Liberties Union. He wanted the organization to work for release of political prisoners, whom he dramatized in the 1924 play *Singing Jailbirds.*

California, "land of orange groves and jails" where this play is written, there are 97 men now in jail, against whom no act of violence has been proved or even charged. Most of these men are in solitary confinement as I write these words. In July, 1923, the writer, accompanied by Mrs. Kate Crane-Gartz, a woman well known for her efforts against the Criminal Syndicalism law, and Mr. Alexander Marky, editor of *Pearson's Magazine,* paid a visit to San Quentin prison, and protested to the warden against the holding of some three score political prisoners, members of the IWW, in solitary confinement. One of these prisoners had broken down under the ferocious conditions of labor in the jute-mill, and the others had declared a strike in sympathy, and had been thrown into the "hole." All pleas on behalf of these men were without avail.

Recently the writer addressed a letter to this same warden, asking for information as to the number of men who had been in solitary

Sinclair's play ran for two months in New York and, besides the production
in India advertised here, was also produced in Germany and France; Sinclair
was one of the best-selling American authors in Europe and Asia at the time.

confinement during the past two years, and the periods of such
confinement. The warden replied that records were kept and were
in charge of the State Board of Prison Directors, who might give
out the facts if they saw fit. A letter to the board requesting this
information was "ordered on file"—that is, the request was denied.
A letter to the governor of the state brought a refusal to direct the
board to furnish it. The secrets of California's prison-hells are with-
held from the public eye by the representatives of the ruling class
now in office.

Do political prisoners die in solitary confinement? Not very
often; for the reason that their dying condition is discovered, and
they are taken to some hospital, thus enabling the prison authorities to deny prison deaths. That is what happened to Paul Bourgon,
IWW, who was among the six hundred men swept into jail at San

Pedro; he was confined in a damp cell, with no blanket, and therefore contracted pneumonia, and was taken to a hospital a few hours before his death. The secretary of the General Defense Committee of Chicago writes that six political prisoners have died in prison, and five went insane, one while in solitary confinement....

———————

As THIS PLAY IS being put into type, an unusual incident occurs. The new chief of police of Los Angeles summons a conference of his captains to discuss the increase of crime, and invites a committee from the American Civil Liberties Union to consult with them. At the end of the discussion Police Captain Plummer stands up and speaks. This is the officer who was in command at San Pedro last year, and who stated: "I broke that strike." He now states as follows—the substance of his remarks being taken down and certified by Rev. Clinton J. Taft, director of the American Civil Liberties Union of Los Angeles, and Mr. J. H. Ryckman, an attorney of Los Angeles. Their summary reads:

"Somebody has been making holy asses of us policemen. Last summer at the time of the harbor strike I went to see old man Hammond. He told me to take a bunch of my men, arm them with clubs, go up on Liberty Hill and break the heads of the Wobblies. I replied that if we did that they would burn down his lumber piles. 'They will do it anyhow,' he answered. But they didn't. Not an overt act have they committed.

"The police who raided the IWW hall in San Pedro recently and threw that piano out in the rain did commit an overt act, however. In fact, we policemen have been made the tools of big business interests of this town who want to run things. I'm ashamed of myself for consenting to do their dirty work.

"It's a good thing I'm not a Wobbly. If I were and had been kept in San Quentin for fourteen months unjustly, as have the Wobblies just discharged because of a reversal of their case in the lower court by decision of the appellate division, I would come out a direct actionist, and hell would be to pay. These Wobblies are better men than we are—they show more self-control.

"The big fellows in this town can do anything they like and get away with it. But the workers can't even think what they want to think without being thrown into jail. This sending men to the pen for things done by Wobblies seven or eight years ago is all wrong— it's an outrage."

And a few days after this speech was made, a mob of three hundred men, including policemen and sailors, raids a peaceful entertainment held in the IWW hall at San Pedro, and beats those present with baseball bats and clubs. One little girl is thrown into a vat of boiling coffee, so that the flesh is cooked from her limbs, and she is in hospital, not expected to live. A number of men are dragged into automobiles, carried out into the country, and tarred and feathered. Repeated appeals to the police authorities in this matter result in promises of arrests but no arrests—excepting for two made by victims of the raid, who met their assailants on the street and escorted them to the police station. Several weeks have passed, but the most determined agitation on the part of the American Civil Liberties Union cannot persuade the public authorities to give any protection to the working people at San Pedro, or any pretense of justice.

Act I, Scene I

Time: The Present.

Place: An Office in the Jail.

At the front of the stage, nearest to the audience, a small room, bare and severe. Entrance center; a flat-topped desk in middle of room, with swivel-chairs on two sides of it; a barred window at right.

At rise: The DISTRICT ATTORNEY sits in chair at right of desk; a smooth-faced, keen-featured lawyer.

"RED" ADAMS stands behind the desk, facing the audience; a lean, wiry, young workingman with pale, tense face, reddish touseled hair, a manner of defiance. He wears old trousers and shirt, no tie.

He does not look at the DISTRICT ATTORNEY, but stares straight before him. Outside, through the window, right, a mob is parading before the jail, singing to the tune of "Hold the Fort for I Am Coming":

> We're here from mine and mill and rail,
>> We're here from off the sea:
> From coast to coast we make the boast
>> Of Solidarity.

From the rear, offstage, comes an answering chorus of several hundred STRIKE-PRISONERS confined in the cells and "tanks" of the jail:

> In California's darkened dungeons
>> For the O. B. U.
> Remember you're outside for us
>> While we're in here for you.

DISTRICT ATTORNEY: Well, this might be a strike we're running, and again it might be a grand opera. *(no answer from the prisoner)* So you're Red Adams?

RED: They call me that.

DISTRICT ATTORNEY: Name Bert, I believe.

RED: Yes.

DISTRICT ATTORNEY: Belong to the IWW

RED: You've got my card at the desk.

DISTRICT ATTORNEY: Give me a straight answer.

RED: I belong to the IWW

DISTRICT ATTORNEY: You understand that I'm the district attorney of this county, and that what you tell me may be used against you?

RED *(looks at DISTRICT ATTORNEY for the first time)*: Mr. 'Cutor, did you ever know a Wobbly to crawl?

DISTRICT ATTORNEY: Out for martyrdom, eh? *(a silence)* You're the leader in this strike?

RED: We don't have leaders in our organization.

DISTRICT ATTORNEY: You've given a few orders, however.

RED: Let your stools tell you about that, Mr. 'Cutor.

DISTRICT ATTORNEY: You're feeling a little sore?

RED: In places. The Chief nearly twisted off my arm this evening.

DISTRICT ATTORNEY: Tried to get away from him?

RED: Hell! You know we never try to get away. You only have to tap us on the shoulder.

THE CROWD (*singing, outside, at the right*):

> We make a pledge—no tyrant might
> > Can make us bend the knee;
> Come on you workers, organize,
> > And fight for Liberty!

THE PRISONERS (*singing in the rear*):

> In California's darkened dungeons
> > For the O. B. U.
> Remember you're outside for us
> > While we're in here for you.

DISTRICT ATTORNEY: Well, Red, you've been having things your own way for the past week.

RED (*laughs*): Ah, Mr. 'Cutor, you don't know what our way is! Some day we'll show you!

DISTRICT ATTORNEY: Dictatorship of the Proletariat, eh? I get you! But meantime you've tied up the ships.

RED: With you loading a dozen a day?

DISTRICT ATTORNEY: Where d'you get that?

RED: I read it in this morning's *Times*.

DISTRICT ATTORNEY: Well, we have to whistle to keep our courage up—the same as you fellows have to sing.

THE CROWD (*outside, singing, to the chorus of "John Brown's Body"*):

> Solidarity forever!
> > Solidarity forever!
> Solidarity forever!
> > And the Union makes us strong!

RED: Well, what's the point? You didn't bring me here to chat on the class struggle.

DISTRICT ATTORNEY: Have a seat, Red. (RED *sits stiffly in chair at left of desk; the* DISTRICT ATTORNEY *takes out cigars*) Have a smoke?

RED: No, thanks.

DISTRICT ATTORNEY: Don't smoke?

RED: Not with parasites.

DISTRICT ATTORNEY: No use to quarrel, Red. Our point of view differs. I think the public has some rights in this harbor.

RED: If you want to talk to me, Mr. 'Cutor, cut out the Sunday school stuff. The public isn't loading these ships—it's the Shipowners' Association. They've given you the orders—over that telephone, I've no doubt. (*a pause*) You see, I know the Dictatorship of the Capitalist Class.

DISTRICT ATTORNEY: Well, my boy, there'll be this much dictatorship—we're going to load the ships.

RED: By arresting all the men who do the work? You must have pinched a thousand tonight.

DISTRICT ATTORNEY: We figure about six hundred.

RED: Well, you go down to the waterfront and take a broom and sweep the harbor dry, and then start to mop up the discontent of the workers.

DISTRICT ATTORNEY: We're going to mop up the agitators and troublemakers——

RED: Troublemakers! Hell, man—get these finks that run the employment business for the Shipowners! You knew how they were robbing the men—you saw us herded there in the slavemarket, showing our muscles to the dealers, trampling each other to get a job! The troublemakers! But shucks—you don't want any preaching from me. You know all the facts. What am I here for? Come to the point!

DISTRICT ATTORNEY: Suppose I just wanted to make the acquaintance of a worthy foe?

RED: Idle curiosity? No, there's something else—and it's something for you, not for me. I wasn't weaned yesterday, Mr. 'Cutor.

DISTRICT ATTORNEY: You were nursed on vinegar, it would seem, Red.

RED: My mother was a working woman—a miner's wife. I guess she got her share of vinegar—the kind your class feeds to my class.

THE CROWD (*shouting outside*):

> Solidarity forever!
>   Solidarity forever!
> Solidarity forever!
>   And the Union makes us strong!

RED: What is it? Come across, man!

DISTRICT ATTORNEY: You know we've got your whole executive committee?

RED: I saw a few of them in my tank.

DISTRICT ATTORNEY: We've got the rest.

RED: Well, there'll be a new committee.

DISTRICT ATTORNEY: They can't give orders without our finding them.

RED: Oh, sure! You'll crush this strike. This is only practice.

DISTRICT ATTORNEY: Don't forget, it's practice for the police also.

RED (*fixes him with an intent look*): Good God, are you figuring to win me over? Make a deal with me—like I was some old line labor leader?

DISTRICT ATTORNEY (*in a business-like tone*): You know Jake Apperson, don't you?

RED: Sure; old pal of mine.

DISTRICT ATTORNEY: You went through the Oakland strike with him?

RED: I sure did.

DISTRICT ATTORNEY: You know he's out of jail again?

RED: I heard it.

DISTRICT ATTORNEY: Expecting him down here?

RED: Ask your spies, Mr. 'Cutor. You'll get nothing like that out of me.

DISTRICT ATTORNEY: Jake Apperson! One of your barn-burning gang!

RED (*starts*): Barn-burning? Cut it out! You aren't such a fool!

DISTRICT ATTORNEY: Oh, you're a choir of lily-white angels, you Wobblies! That's why you sing all the time! Well, you know what you stand to get, Red: criminal syndicalism.

RED: Twenty-eight years—yep.

DISTRICT ATTORNEY: You won't live through that.

RED: Nope.

DISTRICT ATTORNEY (*studying him curiously*): I don't see what you figure to gain.

RED: You don't see, and I couldn't make you see. (*with a laugh*) However, it's more comfortable here than in the tank, so if you're looking for a lecture, you can have it. I've been what you call a leader of the Wobblies for three years. I've traveled from Vancouver to San Diego; I've visited every lumber camp and every harbor on the Pacific Coast. I've talked to the men on the job—there must be ten thousand that know me, and they know I'm not in the business for my pocket. Tonight the word goes out—they've got Red Adams in jail. Pretty soon it'll be: They're trying him in their dirty courts. It'll be: Their bulls and their lousy stools are lying about him. The 'cutor of the Shipowners' Association is accusing him of burning barns. Then it'll be: They've sent up Red Adams for twenty-eight years! They've got him coughing out his lungs in the jute mill! They've got him in the hole—he's hunger-striking, because he wouldn't stand for the beating of some fellow-worker. Then some day it'll be: Red Adams is dead! Red Adams died for us! Do you think they're all skunks and cowards, Mr. 'Cutor? Why, man, when you get through there'll be a thousand on the job in my place!

THE CROWD (*outside, singing*):

> Long-haired preachers come out every night,
>   Try to tell you what's wrong and what's right,
> But when asked how 'bout something to eat,
>   They will answer with voices so sweet.

THE PRISONERS (*at rear, offstage*):

> You will eat,
>> Bye and bye,
>> In that glorious land above the sky.
> Work and pray,
>> Live on hay,
> You'll get pie in the sky when you die!

DISTRICT ATTORNEY: A little comic relief!

RED: You might learn something from that song. Ever hear of Joe Hill? He wrote it. And out in Utah the master-class stood him up against a wall and shot him with a firing-squad. They called him a burglar—just such a frame-up as you'd delight in. But now Joe Hill's songs are all over the land. We sing 'em in Dago and Mex, in Hunkie and Wop, we even sing 'em in Jap and Chink! We're teaching 'em to five or ten thousand tonight—you hear the lessons! In California's darkened dungeons, for the O. B. U. They say: What's the O. B. U.? We answer: The One Big Union! They say: What's the One Big Union? We answer: The IWW! Solidarity for the workers! The hammer that will smash the doors of all the jails!

THE CROWD (*outside, singing*):

> In California's darkened dungeons
>> For the O. B. U.
> Remember you're inside for us
>> While we're out here for you!

RED: Don't you see how you're doing our work, Mr. 'Cutor ?

DISTRICT ATTORNEY: And you're sure you don't want to work for me, Red?

RED: Hey?

DISTRICT ATTORNEY: You know, we could make it easy for you. We could find some trick to let you get away——

RED: Oh! So that's it, after all!

DISTRICT ATTORNEY: We could find you a very good sum of money.

RED: Judas Iscariot, Benedict Arnold, and Red Adams! California for climate, hell for company!

DISTRICT ATTORNEY: A lot of your fellows are getting theirs, you understand. We carry three of your executive committee on our payroll.

RED: That may be true, and again, it may be a shrewd lie to take the heart out of us. We soon spot the ones you get.

DISTRICT ATTORNEY: They become tame and conservative, eh?

RED: Quite the contrary! They become real, sure enough red revolutionists—regular fire-eaters. Want to get something done— maybe burning a barn or two! *(with a smile)* You see, Mr. 'Cutor, we fellows who are nursed on vinegar and go to work at the age of ten—we grow just as sharp wits as you fellows who go to college and live on bootleg whiskey.

DISTRICT ATTORNEY: So, Red, you're bound to fight us!

RED: We nail the IWW preamble to the wall: "We are forming the new society within the shell of the old."

DISTRICT ATTORNEY *(earnestly)*: You're an intelligent man, Red—one of the keenest. Take it from me—this lousy gang isn't worth what you'll suffer for them.

RED: They're just average stiffs, of course; some of them are scum. But they're learning the great lesson, Solidarity; and somebody has to teach it.

DISTRICT ATTORNEY: You weren't always an agitator, I take it.

RED: No, I was an honest workingman. I read the advertisements of your boosters, and came to sunny California, and put my little savings into a ranch. You know what happened when the war was over and prices went down!

DISTRICT ATTORNEY: Married man?

RED: I was then.

DISTRICT ATTORNEY: Where's your wife?

RED: Where you want to put me.

DISTRICT ATTORNEY: In jail?

RED: No—in her grave.

DISTRICT ATTORNEY: I understand you had some children.

RED: Yes, a boy and a girl.

DISTRICT ATTORNEY: Where are they?

RED: They're being taken care of.

DISTRICT ATTORNEY: By you?

RED: No, by others.

DISTRICT ATTORNEY: You support them?

RED: They don't need it.

DISTRICT ATTORNEY: In other words, you deserted them?

RED: Who told you that yarn?

DISTRICT ATTORNEY: You left them to other people so you could go off with some other woman?

RED (*starts*): You dirty cur! Is that what I'm here for—to have you spit on my grief!

DISTRICT ATTORNEY (*sneering*): Looks like I've found a sore spot, eh?

RED: If you weren't a coward, you'd say that outside, where I could knock your block off! You whore-master, with your little stenographer! (*the other clenches his fist as if to strike him*) Oho! You think we didn't hear about the lady that you had in the private room at the roadhouse and the suit she threatened and the dough she got out of you! And you dare to throw my life's tragedy in my face!

DISTRICT ATTORNEY (*coldly*): Well, Red, I guess we won't prolong this discussion.

RED: No—since you're not having it all your own way.

DISTRICT ATTORNEY: You'll find the law will have its way, my man!

RED: To hell with you and your law! Bring on your perjurers and your torturers! Send me up for criminal syndicalism—or choke the life out of me, if you want to! I wipe my feet on you—lackeys and lickspittles of the capitalist class! You and the whole crooked game that you call your law—bribers and bribe-takers——

DISTRICT ATTORNEY: Rave on—we'll stop your foul mouth. (*he presses a button on his desk*)

RED: Yes, you may stop mine—but there are others you'll not stop! (*he rushes to the window and waves his arms through the bars, shouting*) Solidarity for the workers!

THE CROWD: Hooray! It's Red! Red Adams! Red! Red! Three cheers for Red! Hooray for Red! Red! Red! (RED *starts singing to the crowd outside, which takes it up*)

> We speak to you from jail today,
>> Six hundred union men;
> We're here because the bosses' laws
>> Bring slavery again.

(*two police officers enter; the* DISTRICT ATTORNEY *indicates* RED *with a jerk of the thumb, and they collar him and drag him from the room. He sings, in unison with the crowd outside and with the prisoners inside the jail*)

> In California's darkened dungeons
>> For the O. B. U.
> Remember you're outside for us
>> While we're in here for you.

(*the curtain falls; the singing continues until the rise on Scene II. The audience is invited to join the singing*)

———

PASADENA CALIFORNIA, MAY 17, 1923
LOUIS D. OAKS, CHIEF OF POLICE, LOS ANGELES

HAVING ESCAPED FROM your clutches yesterday afternoon, owing to the fact that one of your men betrayed your plot to my wife, I am now in position to answer your formal statement to the public, that I am "more dangerous than 4,000 IWW." I thank you for this compliment, for to be dangerous to lawbreakers in office such as yourself is the highest duty that a citizen of this community can perform.

In the presence of seven witnesses I obtained from Mayor Cryer on Tuesday afternoon the promise that the police would respect my constitutional rights at San Pedro, and that I would not be molested unless I incited to violence. But when I came to you, I learned that you had taken over the mayor's office at the Harbor. Now, from your signed statement to the press, I learn that you have taken over the district attorney's office also; for you tell the public: "I will prosecute Sinclair with all the vigor at my command, and upon his conviction I will demand a jail sentence with hard labor." And you then sent your men to swear to a complaint charging me with "discussing, arguing, orating, and debating certain thoughts and theories, which thoughts and theories were contemptuous of the constitution of the State of California, calculated to cause hatred and contempt of the government of the United States of America, and which thoughts and theories were detrimental and in opposition to the orderly conduct of affairs of business, affecting the rights of private property and personal liberty, and which thoughts and theories were calculated to cause any citizen then and there present and hearing the same to quarrel and fight and use force and violence." And this although I told you at least a dozen times in your office that my only purpose was to stand on private property with the written permission of the owner, and there to read the Constitution of the United States; and you perfectly well know that I did this, and only this, and that three sentences from the Bill of Rights of the Constitution was every word that I was permitted to utter—the words being those which guarantee "freedom of speech and of the press, and the right of the people peaceably to assemble, and to petition the government for the redress of grievances."

But you told me that "this Constitution stuff" does not go at the Harbor. You have established martial law, and you told me that if I tried to read the Constitution, even on private property, I would be thrown into jail, and there would be no bail for me—and this even though I read you the provision of the State constitution guaranteeing me the right to bail....

I charge, and I intend to prove in court, that you are carrying out the conspiracy of the Merchants' and Manufacturers' Association to smash the harbor strike by brutal defiance of law....It is you who are doing the job for [I. H.] Rice [president of the association], and the cruelties you are perpetrating would shock this community if they were known, and they will be punished if there is a God in Heaven to protect the poor and friendless. You did all you could to keep me from contact with the strikers in jail; nevertheless I learned of one horror that was perpetrated only yesterday—fifty men crowded into one small space, and because they committed some slight breach of regulations, singing their songs, they were shut in this hole for two hours without a breath of air, and almost suffocated. Also I saw the food that these men are getting twice a day, and you would not feed it to your dog. And now the city council has voted for money to build a "bull-pen" for strikers, and day by day the public is told that the strike is broken, and the men, denied every civil right, have no place to meet to discuss their policies, and no one to protect them or to protest for them. That is what you want—those are the orders you have got from the Merchants' and Manufacturers' Association; the men are to go back as slaves, and the Constitution of the United States is to cease to exist so far as concerns workingmen.

All I can say, sir, is that I intend to do what little one man can do to awaken the public conscience, and that meantime I am not frightened by your menaces. I am not a giant physically; I shrink from pain and filth and vermin and foul air, like any other man of refinement; also, I freely admit that when I see a line of a hundred policemen with drawn revolvers flung across a street to keep anyone from coming onto private property to hear my feeble voice, I am somewhat disturbed in my nerves. But I have a conscience and a religious faith, and I know that our liberties were not won without suffering, and may be lost again through our cowardice. I intend to do my duty to my country. I have received a telegram from the American Civil Liberties Union in New York, asking me if I will speak at a mass meeting of protest in Los Angeles, and I have answered that I will do so. That meeting will be called at once, and you may come there and hear what the citizens of this community think of your efforts to introduce the legal proceedings of Czarist Russia into our free Republic.

Oil!
1927

> I am devoting all my time and energy to writing a novel about the class struggle in California. This must be accepted as my contribution to the welfare of the California working class.
> —*Upton Sinclair to R. L. Stubble, August 6, 1926*

WHEN *Oil!* WAS BANNED in Boston for its frank discussion of birth control, Sinclair appealed to literary figures for testimonials. D. H. Lawrence wrote: "I read it with keen interest, and consider it a splendid novel in fact."[1] Shortly after *Oil!* was published in 1927, the Julian Petroleum Corporation collapsed after an over-issue of five million dollars in stocks. Tens of thousands lost money as a handful of stockbrokers made large profits. The scandal boosted the sales of *Oil!*.

In Japan, the book was translated in 1930 by Hiroichiro Maedako, who considered it "a political masterpiece exposing capitalism in the field of oil concessions."[2] Sachiko Nakada's 1990 *Japanese Empathy for Upton Sinclair* explains that in Japan the 1920s and 1930s were sometimes labeled "Sinkurea Jidai," meaning "the Sinclair era."[3] She believes that the Sinclair novels changed the mentality of a whole generation, not only in Japan, but in India and China as well. After Sinclair's death in 1968, Ryo Namikawa lamented, "The merry days of America have passed away with him."[4]

There were occasional attempts to keep those merry days alive in California. Robert Hahn, who founded the *Upton Sinclair Quarterly* in 1977, led the most notable effort. In 1980, he and his wife Genevieve produced an adaptation of *Oil!* in Altadena. Sinclair's son, David, attended and photographed their performance. Hahn recalled that "the director's view was that the audience should feel that here was something—the discovery of oil—that was overpowering to people in Los Angeles. It had suddenly become a monster."[5] The audience was put on moveable platforms which were rolled around the theater. Hahn explained:

How to do a gusher on a small stage with very little equipment? It's got to be a psychological kind of thing; the audience has to feel it. So we passed out hard hats—it was hard getting old-fashioned ones, but we did. And we got the tape recorder going, and it all really just "whooshed" up there with a lot of booming sound. And there were people who jumped on ladders and on the stage at different heights and started yelling, warning that the well was coming in. It really got them excited and involved."[6]

In 2001, Word for Word Performing Arts Company presented the first chapter of *Oil!* for rapt audiences in San Francisco.[7] The company commissioned a sculptor to create a giant musical car; in the driver's seat sat Dad. He is often cited as one of the most sympathetic portrayals of a businessman in American literature, but Dad is also a devastating parody of patriarchal authority. This portrait of an "oil man" had astonishing resonance to the audience. Reviewers

When the first chapter of *Oil!* was performed by the Word for Word Performing Arts Company in 2001, reviewer Karen D'Souza wrote in the *San Jose Mercury News*: "The show emerges as a seamless chronicle of a bygone age…the theatre-goer may experience the irresistible impulse to rush out and read the book from cover to cover."

expressed amazement at the grace and irony of Sinclair's writing, and at his intimate and knowing depiction of the lives of the wealthy.[8]

Notes

1. D. H. Lawrence letter, July 16, 1927, quoted in Leon Harris, *Upton Sinclair: American Rebel* (New York: Thomas Crowell, 1975), 241

2. Hiroichiro Maedako, *Bungei Sensen*, December 1927, quoted in Sachiko Nakada, *Japanese Empathy for Upton Sinclair* (Tokyo: Chiyoda-ku, The Central Institute, 1990), 47

3. Nakada, *Japanese Empathy*, 1

4. Ryo Namikawa, "Literary Work of Upton Sinclair," *Eigo Seinen*, February 1969, in Nakada, *Japanese Empathy*, 78

5. John Ahouse interview with Robert Hahn, *Upton Sinclair Quarterly* IV:1, March 1980, 13

6. Ibid., 14

7. Karen D'Souza, *San Jose Mercury News*, January 13, 2001: "The show emerges as a seamless chronicle of a bygone age...when the realization strikes that this pilgrimage through the past is nearing an end, the theatergoer may experience the irresistible impulse to rush out and read the book from cover to cover." For more information contact Word for Word at 1360 Mission St., San Francisco, CA 94102.

8. Robert Hurwitt, *San Francisco Chronicle*, January 14, 2001

CHAPTER 1: THE RIDE

THE ROAD RAN, smooth and flawless, precisely fourteen feet wide, the edges trimmed as if by shears, a ribbon of grey concrete, rolled out over the valley by a giant hand. The ground went in long waves, a slow ascent and then a sudden dip; you climbed, and went swiftly over—but you had no fear, for you knew the magic ribbon would be there, clear of obstructions, unmarred by bump or scar, waiting the passage of inflated rubber wheels revolving seven times a second. The cold wind of morning whistled by, a storm of motion, a humming and roaring with ever-shifting overtones; but you sat snug behind a tilted wind-shield, which slid the gale up over your head. Sometimes you liked to put your hand up, and feel the cold impact; sometimes you would peer around the side of the shield, and let the torrent hit your forehead, and toss your hair about. But for the most part you sat silent and dignified—because that was Dad's way, and Dad's way constituted the ethics of motoring.

Dad wore an overcoat, tan in color, soft and woolly in texture, opulent in cut, double-breasted, with big collar and big lapels and big flaps over the pockets—every place where a tailor could express munificence. The boy's coat had been made by the same tailor, of the same soft, woolly material, with the same big collar and big lapels and big flaps. Dad wore driving gauntlets; and the same shop had had the same kind for boys. Dad wore horn-rimmed spectacles; the boy had never been taken to an oculist, but he had found in a drug-store a pair of amber-colored glasses having horn rims the same as Dad's. There was no hat on Dad's head, because he believed that wind and sunshine kept your hair from falling out; so the boy also rode with tumbled locks. The only difference between them, apart from size, was that Dad had a big brown cigar, unlighted, in the corner of his mouth; a survival of the rough old days, when he had driven mule-teams and chewed tobacco.

Fifty miles, said the speedometer; that was Dad's rule for open country, and he never varied it, except in wet weather. Grades made no difference; the fraction of an ounce more pressure with his right foot, and the car raced on—up, up, up—until it topped the ridge, and was sailing down into the next little valley, exactly in the centre of the magic grey ribbon of concrete. The car would start to gather speed on the down grade, and Dad would lift the pressure of his foot a trifle, and let the resistance of the engine check the speed. Fifty miles was enough, said Dad; he was a man of order.

Far ahead, over the tops of several waves of ground, another car was coming. A small black speck, it went down out of sight, and came up bigger; the next time it was bigger yet; the next time—it was on the slope above you, rushing at you, faster and faster, a mighty projectile hurled out of a six-foot cannon. Now came a moment to test the nerve of a motorist. The magic ribbon of concrete had no stretching powers. The ground at the sides had been prepared for emergencies, but you could not always be sure how well it had been prepared, and if you went off at fifty miles an hour you would get disagreeable waverings of the wheels; you might find the neatly trimmed concrete raised several inches above the earth at the side of it, forcing you to run along on the earth until you could find a place to swing in again; there might be soft sand, which would swerve you this way and that, or wet clay which would skid you, and put a sudden end to your journey.

So the laws of good driving forbade you to go off the magic ribbon except in extreme emergencies. You were ethically entitled to several inches of margin at the right-hand edge; and the man approaching you was entitled to an equal number of inches; which left a remainder of inches between the two projectiles as they shot by. It sounds risky as one tells it, but the heavens are run on the basis of similar calculations, and while collisions do happen, they leave time enough in between for universes to be formed, and successful careers conducted by men of affairs.

"Whoosh!" went the other projectile, hurtling past; a loud, swift "Whoosh!" with no tapering off at the end. You had a glimpse of another man with horn-rimmed spectacles like yourself, with a similar grip of two hands upon a steering wheel, and a similar cataleptic fixation of the eyes. You never looked back; for at fifty miles an hour, your business is with the things that lie before you, and the past is past—or shall we say that the passed are passed? Presently would come another car, and again it would be necessary for you to leave the comfortable centre of the concrete ribbon, and content yourself with a precisely estimated one-half minus a certain number of inches. Each time, you were staking your life upon your ability to place your car upon the exact line—and upon the ability and willingness of the unknown other party to do the same. You watched his projectile in the instant of hurtling at you, and if you saw that he was not making the necessary concession, you knew that you were encountering that most dangerous of all two-legged mammalian creatures, the road-hog. Or maybe it was a drunken man, or just a woman—there was no time to find out; you had the thousandth part of a second in which to shift your steering-wheel the tenth part of an inch, and run your right wheels off onto the dirt.

That might happen only once or twice in the course of a day's driving. When it did, Dad had one invariable formula; he would shift the cigar a bit in his mouth and mutter: "Damn fool!" It was the only cuss-word the one-time mule-driver permitted himself in the presence of the boy; and it had no profane significance—it was simply the scientific term for road-hogs, and drunken men, and women driving cars; as well as for loads of hay, and furniture-vans, and big motor-trucks which blocked the road on curves; and for cars with trailers, driving too rapidly, and swinging from side to side; and for Mexicans in tumble-down buggies, who failed to keep out on the dirt where they belonged, but came wobbling onto the concrete—and right while a car was coming in the other direction, so that you had to jam on your foot-brake, and grab the hand-brake, and bring the car to a halt with a squealing grinding, and worse yet a sliding of tires. If there is anything a motorist considers disgraceful it is to "skid his tires" and Dad had the conviction that some day there would be a speed law turned inside out—it would be forbidden to drive less than forty miles an hour on state highways, and people who wanted to drive spavined horses to tumble-down buggies would either go cross-lots or stay at home.

II

A BARRIER OF MOUNTAINS lay across the road. Far off, they had been blue, with a canopy of fog on top; they lay in tumbled masses, one summit behind another, and more summits peeking over, fainter in color, and mysterious. You knew you had to go up there, and it was interesting to guess where a road might break in. As you came nearer, the great masses changed color—green, or grey, or tawny yellow. No trees grew upon them, but bushes of a hundred shades. They were spotted with rocks, black, white, brown, or red;

also with the pale flames of the yucca, a plant which reared a thick stem ten feet or more in the air, and covered it with small flowers in a huge mass, exactly the shape of a candle flame, but one that never flickered in the wind.

The road began to climb in earnest; it swung around the shoulder of a hill, and there was a sign in red letters: GUADALUPE GRADE: SPEED LIMIT ON CURVES 15 MILES PER HOUR. Dad gave no evidence that he knew how to read, either that sign or his speedometer. Dad understood that signs were for people who did not know how to drive; for the initiate few the rule was, whatever speed left you on your own half of the highway. In this case the road lay on the right side of the pass; you had the mountain on your right, and hugged it closely as you swung round the turns; the other fellow had the outside edge, and in the cheerful phrase of the time, it was "his funeral." Another concession Dad made—wherever the bend was to the right, so that the mass of the mountain obstructed the road, he sounded his horn. It was a big, commanding horn, hidden away somewhere under the capacious hood of the car; a horn for a man whose business took him on flying trips over a district big enough for an ancient empire; who had important engagements waiting at the end of his journey, and who went through, day or night, fair weather or foul. The voice of his horn was sharp and military; there was in it no undertone of human kindness. At fifty miles an hour there is no place for such emotions—what you want is for people to get out of the way, and do it quick, and you tell them so. "Whanhnh!" said the horn—a sound you must make through your nose, for the horn was one big nose. A sudden swing of the highway— "Whanhnh!"—and then an elbow jutting out and another swing —"Whanhnh!"—so you went winding up, up, and the rocky walls of Guadalupe Pass resounded to the strange new cry "Whanhnh! Whanhnh!" The birds looked about in alarm, and the ground squirrels dived into their sandy entrance-holes, and ranchmen driving rickety Fords down the grade, and tourists coming to Southern California with all their chickens and dogs and babies and mattresses and tin pans tied onto the running-boards—these swung out to the last perilous inch of the highway, and the low, swift roadster sped on: "Whanhnh! Whanhnh!"

Any boy will tell you that this is glorious. Whoopee! you bet! Sailing along up there close to the clouds, with an engine full of power, magically harnessed, subject to the faintest pressure from the ball of your foot. The power of ninety horses—think of that! Suppose you had had ninety horses out there in front of you, forty-five pairs in a long line, galloping around the side of a mountain, wouldn't that make your pulses jump? And this magic ribbon of concrete laid out for you, winding here and there, feeling its way upward with hardly a variation of grade, taking off the shoulder of a mountain, cutting straight through the apex of another, diving into the black belly of a third; twisting, turning, tilting inward on the outside curves, tilting outward on the inside curves, so that you were always balanced, always safe—and with a white-painted line marking the centre, so that you always knew exactly where you had a right to be—what magic had done all this?

Dad had explained it—money had done it. Men of money had said the word, and surveyors and engineers had come, and diggers by the thousand, swarming Mexicans and Indians, bronze of skin, armed with picks and shovels; and great steam shovels with long hanging lobster-claws of steel; derricks with wide swinging arms, scrapers and grading machines, steel drills and blasting men with dynamite, rock-crushers, and concrete mixers that ate sacks of cement by the thousand, and drank water from a flour-stained hose, and had round steel bellies that turned all day with a grinding noise. All these had come, and for a year or two they had toiled, and yard by yard they had unrolled the magic ribbon.

Never since the world began had there been men of power equal to this. And Dad was one of them; he could do things like that, he was on his way to do something like that now. At seven o'clock this evening, in the lobby of the Imperial Hotel at Beach City, a man would be waiting, Ben Skutt, the oil-scout, whom Dad described as his "lease-hound"; he would have a big "proposition" all lined up, and the papers ready for signature. So it was that Dad had a right to have the road clear; that was the meaning of the sharp military voice of the horn, speaking through its nose: "Whanhnh! Whanhnh! Dad is coming! Get out of the way! Whanhnh! Whanhnh!"

The boy sat, eager-eyed, alert; he was seeing the world, in a fashion men had dreamed in the days of Haroun al Raschid—from a magic horse that galloped on top of the clouds, from a magic carpet that went sailing through the air. It was a giant's panorama unrolling itself; new vistas opening at every turn, valleys curving below you, hilltops rising above you, processions of ranges, far as your eye could reach. Now that you were in the heart of the range, you saw that there were trees in the deep gorges, towering old pine trees, gnarled by storms and split by lightning; or clumps of live oaks that made pleasant spaces like English parks. But up on the tops there was only brush, now fresh with the brief spring green; mesquite and sage and other desert plants that had learned to bloom quickly, while there was water, and then stand the long baking drought. They were spotted with orange-colored patches of dodder, a plant that grew in long threads like corn silk, weaving a garment on top of the other plants; it killed them but there were plenty more.

Other hills were all rock, of an endless variety of color. You saw surfaces mottled and spotted like the skins of beasts—tawny leopards, and creatures red and grey or black and white, whose names you did not know. There were hills made of boulders, scattered as if giants had been throwing them in battle; there were blocks piled up, as if the children of giants had grown tired of play. Rocks towered like cathedral arches over the road; through such an arch you swung out into view of a gorge, yawning below, with a stout white barrier to protect you as you made the turn. Out of the clouds overhead a great bird came sailing; his wings collapsed as if he had been shot, and he dived into the abyss. "Was that an eagle?" asked the boy. "Buzzard," answered Dad, who had no romance in him.

Higher and higher they climbed, the engine purring softly, one unvarying note. Underneath the wind-shield were dials and gauges in complicated array: a speedometer with a little red line showing exactly how fast you were going; a clock, and an oil gauge, a gas gauge, an ammeter, and a thermometer that mounted slowly on a long grade like this. All these things were in Dad's consciousness— a still more complicated machine. For, after all, what was ninety horse-power compared with a million dollar power? An engine might break down, but Dad's mind had the efficiency of an eclipse of the sun. They were due at the top of the grade by ten o'clock; and the boy's attitude was that of the old farmer with a new gold watch, who stood on his front porch in the early morning, remarking, "If that sun don't get over the hill in three minutes, she's late."

III

BUT SOMETHING WENT wrong and spoiled the schedule. You had got up into the fog, and cold white veils were sweeping your face. You could see all right, but the fog had wet the road, and there was clay on it, a combination that left the most skilful driver helpless. Dad's quick eye noted it, and he slowed down; a fortunate thing, for the car began to slide, and almost touched the white wooden barrier that guarded the outer edge.

They started again, creeping along, in low gear, so that they could stop quickly; five miles the speedometer showed, then three miles; then another slide, and Dad said "Damn." They wouldn't stand that very long, the boy knew; "Chains," he thought, and they drew up close against the side of the hill, on an inside curve where cars coming from either direction could see them. The boy opened the door at his side and popped out; the father descended gravely, and took off his overcoat and laid it in the seat; he took off his coat and laid that in the same way—for clothing was part of a man's dignity, a symbol of his rise in life, and never to be soiled or crumpled. He unfastened his cuffs and rolled up the sleeves—each motion precisely followed by the boy. At the rear of the car was a flat compartment with a sloping cover, which Dad opened with a key; one of a great number of keys, each precisely known to him, each symbolical of efficiency and order. Having got out the chains, and fastened them upon the rear tires, Dad wiped his hands on the fog-laden plants by the roadside; the boy did the same, liking the coldness of the shining globes of water. There was a clean rag in the compartment, kept there for drying your hands, and changed every so often. The two donned their coats again, and resumed their places, and the car set out, a little faster now, but still cautiously, and away off the schedule.

GUADALUPE GRADE: HEIGHT OF LAND: CAUTION: FIFTEEN MILES PER HOUR ON CURVES. So ran the sign; they were creeping down now, in low gear, holding back the car, which resented it, and shook impatiently. Dad had his spectacles in his lap, because the fog had blurred them; it had filled his hair with moisture, and was trickling down his forehead into his eyes. It was fun to breathe it and feel the cold; it was fun to reach over and sound the horn—Dad would let you do it now, all you wanted. A car came creeping towards them out of the mist, likewise tooting lustily; it was a Ford, puffing from the climb, with steam coming out of the radiator.

Then suddenly the fog grew thinner; a few wisps more, and it was gone; they were free, and the car leaped forward into a view—oh, wonderful! Hill below hill dropping away, and a landscape spread out, as far as forever; you wanted wings, so as to dive down there, to sail out over the hilltops and the flat plains. What was the use of speed limits, and curves, and restraining gears and brakes? "Dry my spectacles," said Dad, prosaically. Scenery was all right, but he had to keep to the right of the white-painted line on the road. "Whanhnh! Whanhnh!" said the horn, on all the outside curves.

They slid down, and little by little the scenery disappeared; they were common mortals, back on earth. The curves broadened out, they left the last shoulder of the last hill, and before them was a long, straight descent; the wind began to whistle, and the figures to creep past the red line on the speedometer. They were making up for lost time. Whee! How the trees and telegraph poles went whizzing! Sixty miles now; some people might have been scared, but no sensible person would be scared while Dad was at the wheel.

But suddenly the car began to slow up; you could feel yourself sliding forward in your seat, and the little red line showed fifty, forty, thirty. The road lay straight ahead, there was no other car in sight, yet Dad's foot was on the brake.

The boy looked up inquiringly. "Sit still," said the man. "Don't look round. A speed-trap!"

Oho! An adventure to make a boy's heart jump! He wanted to look and see, but understood that he must sit rigid, staring out in front, utterly innocent. They had never driven any faster than thirty miles per hour in their lives, and if any traffic officer thought he had seen them coming faster down the grade, that was purely an optical delusion, the natural error of a man whose occupation destroyed his faith in human nature. Yes, it must be a dreadful thing to be a "speed-cop," and have the whole human race for your enemy! To stoop to disreputable actions—hiding yourself in bushes, holding a stop-watch in hand, and with a confederate at a certain measured distance down the road, also holding a stop-watch, and with a telephone line connecting the two of them, so they could keep tab on motorists who passed! They had even invented a device of mirrors, which could be set up by the roadside, so that one man could get the flash of a car as it passed, and keep the time. This was a trouble the motorist had to keep incessant watch for; at the slightest sign of anything suspicious, he must slow up quickly—and yet not too quickly—no, just a natural slowing, such as any man would employ if he should discover that he had accidentally, for the briefest moment, exceeded ever so slightly the limits of complete safety in driving.

"That fellow will be following us," said Dad. He had a little mirror mounted in front of his eyes, so that he could keep tab on such enemies of the human race; but the boy could not see into the mirror, so he had to sit on pins and needles, missing the fun.

"Do you see anything?"

"No, not yet; but he'll come; he knows we were speeding. He puts himself on that straight grade, because everybody goes fast at such a place." There you saw the debased nature of the "speed-cop"! He chose a spot where it was perfectly safe to go fast, and where he knew that everyone would be impatient, having been held in so long by the curves up in the mountains, and by the wet roads! That was how much they cared for fair play, those "speed-cops"!

They crept along at thirty miles an hour; the lawful limit in those benighted times, back in 1912. It took all the thrill out of motoring, and it knocked the schedule to pot. The boy had a vision of Ben Skutt, the "lease-hound," sitting in the lobby of the Imperial Hotel at Beach City; there would be others waiting, also—there were always dozens waiting, grave matters of business with "big money" at stake. You would hear Dad at the long distance telephone, and he would consult his watch, and figure the number of miles to be made, and make his appointment accordingly; and then he had to be there—nothing must stop him. If there were a breakdown of the car, he would take out their suit-cases, and lock the car, hail a passing motorist and get a ride to the next town, and there rent the best car he could find—or buy it outright if need be—and drive on, leaving the old car to be towed in and repaired. Nothing could stop Dad!

But now he was creeping along at thirty miles! "What's the matter?" asked the boy, and received the answer: "Judge Larkey!" Oh, sure enough! They were in San Geronimo County, where the terrible judge Larkey was sending speeders to jail! Never would the boy forget that day when Dad had been compelled to put all his engagements aside, and travel back to San Geronimo, to appear in court and be scolded by this elderly autocrat. Most of the time you did not undergo such indignities; you simply displayed your card to the "speed-cop," showing that you were a member of the Automobile Club, and he would nod politely, and hand you a little slip with the amount of your "bail" noted on it, proportioned to the speed you had been caught at; you mailed a check for the amount, and heard and thought no more about it.

But here in San Geronimo County they had got nasty, and Dad had told Judge Larkey what he thought of the custom of setting "speed-traps"—officers hiding in the bushes and spying on citizens; it was undignified, and taught motorists to regard officers of the law as enemies. The judge had tried to be smart, and asked Dad if he had ever thought of the possibility that burglars also might come to regard officers of the law as enemies. The newspapers had put that on the front page all over the state: OIL OPERATOR OBJECTS TO SPEED LAW: J. ARNOLD ROSS SAYS HE WILL CHANGE IT. Dad's friends kidded him about that, but if he stuck it out sooner or later he was going to make them change that law, and sure enough he did, and you owe to him the fact that there are no more "speed-traps," but if officers have to ride the roads in uniform, and if you watch your little mirror, you can go as fast as you please.

IV

THEY CAME TO A little house by the road-side, with a shed that you drove under, and a round-bellied object, half glass and half red paint, that meant gasoline for sale. FREE AIR, read a sign, and Dad drew up, and told the man to take off his chains. The man brought a jack and lifted the car; and the boy, who was always on the ground the instant the car stopped, opened the rear compartment and got out the little bag for the chains to go in. Also he got out the "grease-gun," and unwrapped that. "Grease is cheaper than steel," Dad would say. He had many such maxims, a whole modern Book of Proverbs which the boy learned by heart. It was not that Dad was anxious to save the money; nor was it that he had grease to sell and not steel; it was the general principle of doing things right, of paying respect to a beautiful piece of machinery.

Dad had got out, to stretch his legs. He was a big figure of a man, filling every inch of the opulent overcoat. His cheeks were rosy, and always fresh from the razor; but at second glance you noted little pockets of flesh about his eyes, and a network of wrinkles. His hair was grey; he had had many cares, and was getting old. His features were big and his whole face round, but he had a solid jaw, which he could set in ugly determination. For the most part, however, his expression was placid, rather bovine, and his thoughts came slowly and stayed a long time. On occasions such as the present he would show a genial side—he liked to talk with the plain sort of folks he met along the road, folks of his own sort, who did not notice his extremely crude English; folks who weren't trying to get any money out of him—at least not enough to matter.

He was pleased to tell this man at the "filling station" about the weather up there in the pass; yes, the fog was thick—delayed them quite a bit—bad place for skidding. Lots of cars got into trouble up there, said the man—that soil was adobe, slick as glass; have to trench the road better. Quite a job that, Dad thought—taking off the side of the mountain. The man said the fog was going now— lots of "high fog" in the month of May, but generally it cleared up by noon. The man wanted to know if Dad needed any gas, and Dad said no, they had got a supply before they tackled the grade. The truth was, Dad was particular, he didn't like to use any gas but his own make; but he wouldn't say that to the man, because it might hurt the man's feelings.

He handed the man a silver dollar for his services, and the man started to get change, but Dad said never mind the change; the man was quite overwhelmed by that, and put up his finger in a kind of salute, and it was evident he realized he was dealing with a "big man." Dad was used to such scenes, of course, but it never failed to bring a little glow to his heart; he went about with a supply of silver dollars and half dollars jingling in his pocket, so that all with whom he had dealings might share that spiritual warmth. "Poor devils," he would say, "they don't get much." He knew, because he had been one of them, and he never lost an opportunity to explain it to the boy. To him it was real, and to the boy it was romantic.

Behind the "filling station" was a little cabinet, decorously marked, "Gents." Dad called this the "emptying station," and that was a joke over which they chuckled. But it was a strictly family joke, Dad explained; it must not be passed on, for other people would be shocked by it. Other people were "queer"; but just why they were queer was something not yet explained.

They took their seats in the car, and were about to start, when who should come riding up behind them—the "speed-cop"! Yes, Dad was right, the man had been following them, and he seemed to scowl when he saw them. They had no business with him, so they drove on; doubtless he would take the filling station as a place to hide, and watch for speeders, said Dad. And so it proved. They had gone for a mile or two, at their tiresome pace of thirty, when a horn sounded behind them, and a car went swiftly by. They let it go, and half a minute later Dad, looking into his little mirror, remarked: "Here comes the cop!" The boy turned round, and saw the motorcycle pass them with a roaring of the engine. The boy leaped up and down in the seat. "It's a race! It's a race! Oh, Dad, let's follow them!"

Dad was not too old to have some sporting spirit left; besides, it was a convenience to have the enemy out in front, where you could watch him, and he couldn't watch you. Dad's car leaped forward, and the figures again crept past the red line of the speedometer—thirty-five—forty—forty-five—fifty—fifty-five. The boy was half lifted out of his seat, his eyes shining and his hands clenched.

The concrete ribbon had come to an end; there was now a dirt road, wide and level, winding in slow curves through a country of gentle hills, planted in wheat. The road was rolled hard, but there were little bumps, and the car leaped from one to another; it was armed with springs and shock-absorbers and "snubbers," every invented device for easy riding. Out in front were clouds of dust, which the wind seized and swept over the hills; you would have thought that an army was marching there. Now and then you got a glimpse of the speeding car, and the motor-cycle close behind it. "He's trying to get away! Oh, Dad, step on her!" This was an adventure you didn't meet on every trip!

"Damn fool!" was Dad's comment; a man who would risk his life to avoid paying a small fine. You couldn't get away from a traffic-officer, at least not on roads like this. And sure enough, the dust clouds died, and on a straight bit of the highway, there they were—the car drawn up at the right, and the officer standing alongside, with his little note-book and pencil, writing things. Dad slowed down to the innocent thirty miles and went by. The boy would have liked to stop, and listen to the argument inevitable on such occasions; but he knew that the schedule took precedence, and here was the chance to make a "get-away." Passing the first turn, they hit it up; the boy looked round every half minute for the next half hour, but they saw no more of the "speed-cop." They were again their own law.

V

SOME TIME AGO these two had witnessed a serious traffic accident, and afterwards had appeared to testify concerning it. The clerk of the court had called "J. Arnold Ross," and then, just as solemnly, "J. Arnold Ross, junior," and the boy had climbed into the witness-chair, and testified that he knew the nature of an oath, and knew the traffic regulations, and just what he had seen.

That had made him, as you might say, "court-conscious." Whenever, in driving, anything happened that was the least bit irregular, the boy's imagination would elaborate it into a court scene. "No, your honor, the man had no business on the left side of the road; we were too close to him, he had no time to pass the car in front of him." Or it was: "Your honor, the man was walking on the right side of the road at night, and there was a car coming towards us that had blinding lights. You know, your honor, a man should walk on the left side of the road at night, so that he can see the cars coming towards him." In the midst of these imaginings of accidents, the boy would give a little jump; and Dad would ask, "What's the matter, son?" The boy would be embarrassed, because he didn't like to say that he had been letting his dreams run away with him. But Dad knew, and would smile to himself; funny kid, always imagining things, his mind jumping from one thing to another, always excited!

Dad's mind was not like that; it got on one subject and stayed there, and ideas came through it in slow, grave procession; his emotions were like a furnace that took a long time to heat up. Sometimes on these drives he would say nothing for a whole hour; the stream of his consciousness would be like a river that has sunk down through rocks and sand, clean out of sight; he would be just a pervading sense of well-being, wrapped in an opulent warm overcoat, an accessory, you might say, of a softly purring engine running in a bath of boiling oil, and traversing a road at fifty miles an hour. If you had taken this consciousness apart, you would have found not thoughts, but conditions of physical organs, and of the weather, and of the car, and of bank-accounts, and of the boy at his side. Putting it into words makes it definite and separate—so you must try to take it all at once, blended together: "I, the driver of this car, that used to be Jim Ross, the teamster, and J. A. Ross and Co., general merchandise at Queen Centre, California, am now J. Arnold Ross, oil operator, and my breakfast is about digested, and I am a little too warm in my big new overcoat because the sun is coming out, and I have a new well flowing four thousand barrels at Lobos River, and sixteen on the pump at Antelope, and I'm on my way to sign a lease at Beach City, and we'll make up our schedule in the next couple of hours, and 'Bunny' is sitting beside me, and he is well and strong, and is going to own everything I am making, and follow in my footsteps, except that he will never make the ugly blunders or have the painful memories that I have, but will be wise and perfect and do everything I say."

Meantime the mind of "Bunny" was not behaving in the least like this, but on the contrary was leaping from theme to theme, as a grass-hopper in a field leaps from one stalk of grass to another. There was a jackrabbit, racing away like mad; he had long ears, like a mule, and why were they so transparent and pink? There was a butcher-bird, sitting on the fence; he stretched his wings all the time, like he was yawning—what did he mean by that? And there was a road-runner, a long lean bird as fast as a race-horse, beautiful and glossy, black and brown and white, with a crest and a streaming tail. Where do you suppose he got water in these dry hills? There on the road was a mangled corpse—a ground squirrel had tried to cross, and a car had mashed it flat; other cars would roll over it, till it was ground to powder and blown away by the wind. There was no use saying anything to Dad about that—he would remark that squirrels carried plague, or at least they had fleas which did; every now and then there would be cases of this disease and the newspapers would have to hush it up, because it was bad for real estate.

But the boy was thinking about the poor little mite of life that had been so suddenly snuffed out. How cruel life was; and how strange that things should grow, and have the power to make themselves, out of nothing apparently—and Dad couldn't explain it, and said that nobody else could, you were just here. And then came a ranch wagon in front of them, a one-sided old thing loaded with household goods; to Dad it was just an obstacle, but "Bunny" saw two lads of his own age, riding in back of the load and staring at him with dull, listless eyes. They were pale, and looked as if they hadn't enough to eat; and that was another thing to wonder about, why people should be poor and nobody to help them. It was a world you had to help yourself in, was Dad's explanation.

"Bunny," the every-day name of this boy, had been started by his mother when he was little—because he was soft and brown and warm, and she had dressed him in a soft, fuzzy sweater, brown in color with white trimmings. Now he was thirteen, and resented the name, but the boys cut it to "Bun," which was to stay with him, and which was satisfactory. He was a pretty boy, still brown, with wavy brown hair, tumbled by the wind, and bright brown eyes, and a good color, because he lived outdoors. He did not go to school, but had a tutor at home, because he was to take his father's place in the world, and he went on these rides in order that he might learn his father's business.

Wonderful, endlessly wonderful, were these scenes; new faces, new kinds of life revealed. There came towns and villages—extraordinary towns and villages, full of people and houses and cars and horses and signs. There were signs along the road; guide-posts at every crossing, giving you a geography lesson—a list of the places to which the roads led, and the distances; you could figure your schedule, and that was a lesson in arithmetic! There were traffic signs, warning you of danger—curves, grades, slippery places, intersections, railroad crossings. There were big banners across the highway, or signs with letters made of electric lights: LOMA VISTA: WELCOME TO OUR CITY. Then, a little farther on: LOMA VISTA, CITY LIMITS: GOOD-BYE: COME AGAIN.

Also there were no end of advertising signs, especially contrived to lend variety to travel. PICTURE AHEAD; KODAK AS YOU GO, was a frequent legend, and you looked for the picture, but never could be sure what it was. A tire manufacturer had set up big wooden figures of a boy waving a flag; Dad said this boy looked like Bunny, and Bunny said he looked like a picture of Jack London he had seen in a magazine. Another tire manufacturer had a great open book, made of wood, and set up at a turn of the road leading into each town; it was supposed to be a history book, and told you something about that place—facts at once novel and instructive: you learned that Citrus was the location of the first orange grove in California, and that Santa Rosita possessed the finest radium springs west of the Rocky Mountains, and that on the outskirts of Crescent City Father Junipero Serra had converted two thousand Indians to Christianity in the year 1769.

There were people still engaged in converting, you learned; they had gone out on the highway with pots of vari-colored paint, and had decorated rocks and railway culverts with inscriptions: PREPARE TO MEET THY GOD. Then would come a traffic sign: RAILROAD CROSSING. STOP. LOOK. LISTEN. The railroad company wanted you to meet your God through some other agency, Dad explained, because there would be damage suits for taking religious faith too seriously. JESUS WAITS, a boulder would proclaim; and then would come, CHICKEN DINNER, $1. There were always funny signs about things to eat—apparently all the world loved a meal, and became jolly at the thought. "Hot Dog Kennels," was an eating-place, and "Ptomaine Tommy," and "The Clam-Baker," and the "Lobster-Pot."

There were endless puns on the word inn—"Dew Drop Inn" and "Happen Inn," "Welcome Inn" and "Hurry Inn." When you went into these places you would find the spirit of jollity rampaging on the walls: IN GOD WE TRUST, ALL OTHERS CASH. DON'T COMPLAIN ABOUT OUR COFFEE; SOME DAY YOU MAY BE OLD AND WEAK YOURSELF. WE HAVE AN ARRANGEMENT WITH OUR BANK; THE BANK DOES NOT SELL SOUP, AND WE DO NOT CASH CHECKS.

VI

THEY WERE PASSING through a broad valley, miles upon miles of wheat fields, shining green in the sun; in the distance were trees, with glimpses of a house here and there. ARE YOU LOOKING FOR A HOME? inquired a friendly sign. "Santa Ynez is a place for folks. Good water, cheap land, seven churches. See Sprouks and Knuckleson, Realtors." And presently the road broadened out, with a line of trees in the middle, and there began to be houses on each side. DRIVE SLOW AND SEE OUR CITY; DRIVE FAST AND SEE OUR JAIL, proclaimed a big board—BY ORDER OF THE MUNICIPAL COUNCIL OF SANTA YNEZ. Dad slowed down to twenty-five miles; for it was a favorite trick of town marshals and justices of the peace to set speed-traps for motorists coming from the country, with engines keyed up to country rates of speed; they would haul you up and soak you a big fine— and you had a vision of these new-style highwaymen spending your dollars in riotous living. That was something else Dad was going to stop, he said—such fines ought to go to the state, and be used for road-repairs.

BUSINESS ZONE, 15 MILES PER HOUR. The main street of Santa Ynez was a double avenue, with two lines of cars parked obliquely in the centre of it, and another line obliquely against each curb. You crept along through a lane, watching for a car that was backing out, and you dived into the vacant place, just missing the fender of the car at your right. Dad got out, and took off his overcoat, and folded it carefully, outside in, the sleeves inside; that was something he was particular about, having kept a general store, which included

"Gents' Clothing." He and Bunny laid their coats neatly in the rear compartment, locked safe, and then strolled down the sidewalk, watching the ranchers of Santa Ynez valley, and the goods which the stores displayed for them. This was the United States, and the things on sale were the things you would have seen in store-windows on any other Main Street, the things known as "nationally advertised products." The ranchman drove to town in a nationally advertised auto, pressing the accelerator with a nationally advertised shoe; in front of the drug-store he found a display of nationally advertised magazines, containing all the nationally advertised advertisements of the nationally advertised articles he would take back to the ranch.

There were a few details which set this apart as a Western town: the width of the street, the newness of the stores, the shininess of their white paint, and the net-work of electric lights hung over the centre of the street; also a man with a broad-brimmed hat, and a stunted old Indian mumbling his lips as he walked, and a solitary cowboy wearing "chaps." ELITE CAFE, said a white-painted sign, reading vertically; the word WAFFLES was painted on the window, and there was a menu tacked by the door, so that you could see what was offered, and the prices charged. There were tables along one side of the wall, and a counter along the other, with a row of broad backs in shirtsleeves and suspenders perched on top of little stools; this was the way if you wanted quick action, so Dad and the boy took two stools they found vacant.

Dad was in his element in a place like this. He liked to "josh" the waitress; he knew all kinds of comic things to say, funny names for things to eat. He would order his eggs "sunny side up," or "with their eyes open, please." He would say, "Wrap the baby in the blanket," and laugh over the waitress' effort to realize that this meant a fried egg sandwich. He would chat with the rancher at his other side—learning about the condition of the wheat, and the prospects of prices for the orange and walnut crops; he was interested in everything like this, as a man who had oil to sell, to men who would buy more or less, according to what they got for their products. Dad owned land, too; he was always ready to "pick up" a likely piece, for there was oil all over Southern California, he said, and some day there would be an empire here.

But now they were behind their schedule, and no time for play. Dad would take fried rabbit; and Bunny thought he wouldn't—not because of the cannibalistic suggestion, but because of one he had seen mashed on the road that morning. He chose roast pork—not having seen any dead pigs. So there came on a platter two slices of meat, and mashed potatoes scooped out in a round ball, with a hole in the top filled with gluey brown gravy; also a spoonful of chopped up beets, and a leaf of lettuce with apple sauce in it. The waitress had given him an extra helping, because she liked this jolly brown kid, with his rosy cheeks and hair tumbled by the wind, and sensitive lips, like a girl's, and eager brown eyes that roamed over the place and took in everything, the signs on the wall, the bottles of catsup and slices of pie, the fat jolly waitress, and the tired thin one who was waiting on him. He cheered her up by telling her about the speed-cop they had met, and the chase they had seen. In turn she tipped them off to a speed-trap just outside the town; the man next to Bunny had been caught in it and fined ten dollars, so they had plenty to talk about while Bunny finished his dinner, and his slice of raisin pie and glass of milk. Dad gave the waitress a half dollar for a tip, which was an unheard-of thing at a counter, and seemed almost immoral; but she took it.

They drove carefully until they were past the speed-trap; then they "hit it up," along a broad boulevard known as the Mission Way, with bronze bells hanging from poles along it. They had all kinds of picturesque names for highways in this country; the Devil's Garden Way and the Rim of the World Drive, Mountain Spring Grade and Snow Creek Run, Thousand Palm Cañon and Fig Tree John's Road, Coyote Pass and the Jackrabbit Trail. There was a Telegraph Road, and that was thrilling to the boy because he had read about a battle in the Civil War for the possession of a "Telegraph Road";

when they drove along this one, he would see infantry hiding in the bushes and cavalry charging across the fields; he would give a start of excitement, and Dad would ask, "What is it?" "Nothing, Dad; I was just thinking." Funny kid! Always imagining things!

Also, there were Spanish names, reverently cherished by the pious realtors of the country. Bunny knew what these meant, because he was studying Spanish, so that some day he would be equipped to deal with Mexican labor. "El Camino Real"—that meant the Royal Highway; and "Verdugo Cañon"—that meant "executioner." "What happened there, Dad?" But Dad didn't know the story; he shared the opinion of the manufacturer of a nationally advertised automobile—that history is mostly "bunk."

VII

THE ROAD WAS asphalt now; it shimmered in the heat, and whenever it fell away before you, a mirage made it look like water. It was lined with orange-groves; dark green shiny trees, golden with a part of last year's crop, and snowy white with the new year's blossoms. Now and then a puff of breeze blew out, and you got a ravishing sweet odor. There were groves of walnuts, broad trees with ample foliage, casting dark shadows on the carefully cultivated, powdery brown soil. There were hedges of roses, extending for long distances, eight or ten feet high, and covered with blossoms. There were wind-breaks of towering thin eucalyptus trees, with long wavy leaves and bark that scales off and leaves them naked; all the world is familiar with them in the moving pictures, where they do duty for sturdy oaks and ancient elms and spreading chestnuts and Arabian date-palms and cedars of Lebanon and whatever else the scenario calls for.

You had to cut your speed down here, and had to watch incessantly; there were intersections, and lanes coming in, and warning signs of many sorts; there was traffic both ways, and delicate decisions to be made as to whether you could get past the car ahead of you before one coming in the other direction would bear down on you and shut you in a pair of scissors. It was exciting to watch Dad's handling of these emergencies, to read his intentions and watch him carry them out.

There were towns every five or ten miles now, and you were continually being slowed up by traffic, and continually being warned to conform to a rate of movement which would have irritated an able-bodied snail. The highway passed through the main street of each town; the merchants arranged that, Dad said, hoping you would get out and buy something at their places; if the highway were shifted to the outskirts of the town, to avoid traffic congestion, all the merchants would forthwith move to the highway! Sometimes they would put up signs, indicating a turn in the highway, attempting to lure the motorist onto a business street; after you had got to the end of that street, they would steer you back to the highway! Dad noted such tricks with the amused tolerance of a man who had worked them on others, but did not let anyone work them on him.

Each town consisted of some tens, or hundreds, or thousands of perfectly rectangular blocks, divided into perfectly rectangular lots, each containing a strictly modern bungalow, with a lawn and a housewife holding a hose. On the outskirts would be one or more "subdivisions," as they were called; "acreage" was being laid out into lots, and decorated with a row of red and yellow flags fluttering merrily in the breeze; also a row of red and yellow signs which asked questions and answered them with swift efficiency: GAS? YES. WATER? BEST EVER. LIGHTS? RIGHT. RESTRICTIONS? YOU BET. SCHOOLS? UNDER CONSTRUCTION. SCENERY? BEATS THE ALPS—and so on. There would be an office or a tent by the roadside, and in front of it an alert young man with a writing pad and a fountain-pen, prepared to write you a contract of sale after two minutes' conversation. These subdividers had bought the land for a thousand dollars an acre, and soon as they had set up the fluttering little flags and the tent it became worth $1675 per lot. This also Dad explained with amused tolerance. It was a great country!

They were coming to the outskirts of Angel City. Here were trolley tracks and railroads, and subdivisions with no "restrictions"—

that is, you might build any kind of house you pleased, and rent it to people of any race or color; which meant an ugly slum, spreading like a great sore, with shanties of tin and tar-paper and unpainted boards. There were great numbers of children playing here—for some strange reason there seemed to be more of them where they were least apt to thrive.

By dint of constant pushing and passing every other car, Dad had got on his schedule again. They skirted the city, avoiding the traffic crowds in its centre, and presently came a sign: BEACH CITY BOULEVARD. It was a wide asphalt road, with thousands of speeding cars, and more subdivisions and suburban home-sites, with endless ingenious advertisements designed to catch the fancy of the motorist, and cause him to put on brakes. The real estate men had apparently been reading the Arabian Nights and Grimm's fairy-tales; they were housed in little freak offices that shot up to a point, or tilted like a drunken sailor; their colors orange and pink, or blue and green, or with separately painted shingles, spotted with various colors. There were GOOD EATS signs and BARBECUE signs—the latter being a word which apparently had not been in the spelling-books when the sign-painters went to school. There were stands where you got orange-juice and cider, with orange-colored wicker chairs out in front for you to sit in. There were fruit and vegetable stands kept by Japs, and other stands with signs inviting you to PATRONIZE AMERICANS. There was simply no end of things to look at, each separate thing bringing its separate thrill to the mind of a thirteen-year-old boy. The infinite strangeness and fascinatingness of this variegated world! Why do people do this, Dad? And why do they do that?

They came to Beach City, with its wide avenue along the ocean-front. Six-thirty, said the clock on the car's running-board—exactly on the schedule. They stopped before the big hotel, and Bunny got out of the car, and opened the back compartment, and the bell-hop came hopping—you bet, for he knew Dad, and the dollars and half dollars that were jingling in Dad's pockets. The bell-hop grabbed the suit-cases and the overcoats, and carried them in, and the boy followed, feeling responsible and important, because Dad couldn't come yet, Dad had to put the car in a parking place. So Bunny strode in and looked about the lobby for Ben Skutt, the oil-scout, who was Dad's "lease-hound." There he was, seated in a big leather chair, puffing at a cigar and watching the door; he got up when he saw Bunny, and stretched his long, lean body, and twisted his lean, ugly face into a grin of welcome. The boy, very erect, remembering that he was J. Arnold Ross, junior, and representing his father in an important transaction, shook hands with the man, remarking: "Good evening, Mr. Skutt. Are the papers ready?"

The Land of Orange Groves and Jails
from "The Open Forum," 1929

IF CALIFORNIA HISTORY texts tend to give scant coverage to the struggles of the Wobblies, they decidedly omit stories like the one Sinclair reports here.[1] In this account, Sinclair describes the role of what he calls "parlor reds" (wealthy liberal sympathizers) in effectively advocating for arrested radical teachers. His own model for a "parlor red" was close confidante Kate Crane-Gartz, who used her inherited fortune to defend activists in causes ranging from labor to civil liberties, as did many of Sinclair's literary protagonists. The lives of Kate Crane-Gartz and another close friend of Sinclair's, Gaylord Wilshire, represented a powerful impulse among wealthy Americans in the early part of the twentieth century.[2]

Sinclair was especially interested in the dilemma of the educated and wealthy American with a social conscience. His heroes from *Oil!* (1927) to *World's End* (1940) embody this contradiction. The hero of *Boston* is a wealthy woman (clearly modeled on Kate Crane-Gartz) who is radicalized by her thwarted efforts to save the radical immigrants Sacco and Vanzetti from being executed for murder and robbery in 1927.[3] Gartz was also the model for the employer in

Another Pamela, 1950, a variation on Samuel Richardson's classic novel *Pamela*.[4] A series of letters from a young servant in a wealthy California household, *Another Pamela* also includes mention of the 1929 arrest of San Bernardino teachers that sparked "The Land of Orange Groves and Jails." Evidently their story continued to haunt Upton Sinclair more than twenty years after it took place.

Scholar Judy Branfman is researching the San Bernardino arrest, motivated by the involvement of her great-aunt Yetta Stromberg, the chief defendant in the ensuing trial. Stromberg was a teacher at a summer camp for workers' children in Yucaipa, California. These radical summer camps had started in the mid 1920s on the East Coast; by 1927, there were a dozen across the country, including the one in San Bernardino County.[5] Branfman reports that Stromberg was harassed by the FBI from the time of her arrest through the following thirty years and was blacklisted from jobs in public schools. The government targeted these teachers as part of the anti-Communist persecution that began with the Palmer raids.

Notes

1. See Richard Rice, William Bullough, and Richard Orsi, *The Elusive Eden* (New York: McGraw Hill, 2002), 5, in which the authors note that during the last century, California and boosterism have often been linked with the "traditional and safe themes of growth, progress, success, social equality, and exciting romance."

2. For more on Sinclair heroes, see Arun Pant, "The Little Narrow Circle of Consciousness: Pink Prototype in Upton Sinclair," in Dieter Herms, ed., *Upton Sinclair: Literature and Social Reform* (Frankfurt: Peter Lang, 1990). For a writing fellowship which enabled me to prepare these materials, I would like to thank Peter Barnes, who, in the tradition of Kate Crane-Gartz, established the Mesa Refuge to allow writers the time to complete our work.

3. A new edition of *Boston* was published in 1978 with an introduction by Howard Zinn (Cambridge, Mass.: Robert Bentley, 1978).

4. Upton Sinclair, *Another Pamela* (New York: Viking Press, 1950). For a discussion of the connection with Kate Crane-Gartz, see John Ahouse, *Upton Sinclair: A Descriptive, Annotated Bibliography* (Los Angeles: Arundel Press, 1994), 115.

5. Personal interview, Judy Branfman, research scholar, UCLA Study for the Center for Women; Branfman is producing a film on *Stromberg v. California*. See also Paul Mishler, *Raising Reds* (New York: Columbia University Press, 1999).

S OUTHERN CALIFORNIA is proud of the above title, first conferred upon it by the "Wobblies" during the criminal syndicalist prosecutions. Southern California has now acquired another lot of political prisoners, and this time the glory of the achievement accrues to the population of the "orange belt." What a sense of security and relief must be in the homes of orange growers this morning when they open their beloved *Times,* and read that five Russian Jewish working-women have been sentenced to San Quentin, one for a period of from one to ten years, and the other four from six months to five years, for the felony of conducting a summer-camp for working children with the flag of Soviet Russia flying over it!

I witnessed the scene in the court room, full of court officers and district attorneys and detectives and "red squad" and Better America Federation agents and reporters of Los Angeles newspapers, and it pleased me so that I wish to spread its fame to the farthest corners of the civilized world. Friends and comrades In New York and London and Paris and Berlin and Stockholm and Amsterdam and Moscow and Tokyo and Sydney and Johannesburg who will read these words, join with me in acclaiming the courage and loyalty to duty of our "heaven-born band" of patriots who saved the orange country from the peril of five Russian Jewish working-girls and a little piece of red silk, home cut and home sewed by the fingers of working-class children! Many glorious events are set forth in our patriotic annals—Concord, with its shot heard round the world, and Bunker Hill, where we trusted in God but kept our powder dry—but nothing, I am sure, can claim a higher place in history's roll than the raid upon the Yucaipa camp by the Better America Federation of Southern California.

It seems that some working people of the east side of Los Angeles, Communists or sympathizers, wanted a place to send their children for a glimpse of the country in summer time, at a cost not too far

Kate Crane-Gartz was one of the Sinclairs' closest friends through the
1920s and 1930s. Sinclair's stable marriage allowed him to have authentic and
supportive friendships with many women, including Margaret Sanger
and Edith Summers Kelly.

beyond their means. They rented a shack at Yucaipa in the mountains of San Bernardino County, sixty-five miles from Los Angeles,
and a group of half a dozen women, with one man to chop wood
and do the heavy work, took care of two score children at a price of
six dollars a week each. The teacher of the camp was Yetta Stromberg,
nineteen years of age, recently a student of the loose University of
California. The name "Comrade Yetta" comes with a familiar sound,
because Arthur Bullard wrote a novel by that title some twenty years
ago; now here is his heroine—except that times have changed and
she calls herself Communist instead of Socialist.

She is, I should estimate, something less than five feet in height,
and if she weighs a hundred pounds I am a bad guesser. She has
quaint little old-fashioned features of delicate loveliness which
would charm a painter of miniatures; and she has a faith which has

caused some to hail her as the "Joan of Arc of Los Angeles." Now she will no longer study social problems in the University of California, but in a more realistic school, the women's department of San Quentin prison, along with hammer murderesses and boot-leg queens and dope fiends. She received a double sentence, because of the very special and aggravating series of crimes which were proved against her in the Superior Court of San Bernardino County.

Yetta, it seems, taught the children history. She taught them that there had been various stages in the development of human soci-ety, tribalism, barbarism, feudalism, capitalism. She had got almost through with the first two, so she testified, and intended to go on to the others, and wind up with her conception of Communism, which she hopes will be the next stage of human evolution. As a preliminary, to prepare the children's minds, she got some red cloth and they made a flag, and with water-colors painted on it a hammer and a sickle. The red symbolized human brotherhood, because of the fact that all human blood is red—excluding, of course, that of patriots and supporters of the Better America Federation, which is blue. The hammer stood for the workers and the sickle for the peas-ants of Russia—it being the idea that farmers and workers should unite to have a government for their own benefit, instead of for the benefit of landlords, capitalists, and bankers, as in America. Every morning the children raised the flag and made a pledge—which was read over and over in court, and constituted the special aggra-vation which brought the double conviction by the brave jury, and the double sentence by the conscientious judge. The pledge read as follows:

> I pledge allegiance to the worker's red flag
> And to the cause for which it stands:
> One aim throughout our lives,
> Freedom for the working class.

So long as Yetta and her children were let alone, the above words were heard only by some fifty persons. But news of her doings leaked out to the noble band of American Legion men who guard the cause of patriotism in San Bernardino. From them it spread to the Better America Federation in Los Angeles, with the result that the camp was raided, and the evil words were repeated before a crowded court room day after day, and were published in all our Southern California newspapers. They are now reproduced in this narrative, and will be read in New York, London, Paris, Berlin, Stockholm, Amsterdam, Moscow, Tokyo, Sydney, and Johannesburg. A campaign in defense of Comrade Yetta will go on in all these cities, and the formula which she taught to a handful of children will be recited and discussed by countless millions of workers. Here is a singularly beautiful illustration of what happens when we set out to suppress ideas by means of policemen's clubs and jails! The demonstration should be of the greatest help to the Better America Federation in its next campaign to raise funds among our bankers and business men.

A gallant band of strapping six-footers, county sheriff's men, American Legion heroes, and red-hunters of the "Intelligence Bureau" of the Los Angeles police department swooped down upon that little camp and carried half a dozen children off to a detention home. Six women and one man, who chopped the wood, were shut up in the San Bernardino jail, and Mr. Leo Gallagher, an attorney of Los Angeles, member of the executive committee of our Civil Liberties Union, went out to arrange for their bail, and in the sheriff's office a deputy sheriff seized him by the throat and choked him.

I took occasion to report this assault to the so-called "Constitutional Rights Committee" of the Los Angeles Bar Association, which referred the matter to the similar committee in San Bernardino County, which in turn did nothing.

In due course the prisoners were brought to trial before Judge Charles L. Allison. John Beardsley, another attorney of Los Angeles—not a radical, but a member of our Civil Liberties group—defended the prisoners, and after a trial lasting nine days, "Comrade Yetta" was convicted on two counts, and four women and one man upon one count, "conspiracy to display a red flag or other emblem of opposition to organized government." The women are Emma Schneiderman, Jennie Wolfson, Esther Karpiloff, and Bella Mintz. It is interesting to note that there was one man from Holland on the jury, C. F. De Meyer, and he held it up for twenty-three hours, and forced the acquittal of Mrs. Schneiderman's mother, who had arrived at the camp just a few hours before the raid. The mother then applied to Mr. Beardsley to be allowed to take her daughter's place in jail!

As a sample of the fairness of the trial it should suffice to record that the sole man at the camp was a veteran of the World War, severely injured by gas in the trenches, and partly incapacitated as a result; and that the jury of patriots of the orange country were denied an opportunity to know that this man was a war veteran, and so they convicted him. Isidor Berkowitz would now be on his road to San Quentin, save that he found a way to deliver himself from the clutches of patriotism. On the night before he was scheduled to be sentenced to San Quentin, he took a rope and hanged himself.

Picture the band of five female felons, assembled in court to hear their fates: all of them frail, and only one of them what we should call a woman of normal stature. They face the stern judge and he questions each in turn. All but one were born in Russia, only two have had a school education, two or three are mothers of children who were in the camp, and the others self-supporting. None of them uses dope, they state in answer to questions, and none has ever been previously convicted of a felony. The two who are members of the Communist party of course refuse to apply for probation; the other three do apply, and the judge turns down the application, on the ground that they are not persons who would be reformed by receiving a new chance. Then he sentences them, and I observe the signs of satisfaction among the four representatives of the Los Angeles "red squad," who have supervised the entire procedure. I do not observe the representative of the Better America Federation, who for some reason desires to keep secret his part in the affair. Mr.

Wainess is his name, and at the trial all those who gave evidence for the state concerning the raid perjured themselves as to his presence; it wasn't until the attorney for the defense put the district attorney on the stand that it was definitely established that Mr. Wainess took part in the raid.

Another court proceeding followed immediately. We have in Southern California a lady by the name of Kate Crane-Gartz, who is what the Better America Federation calls a "parlor red." She is one of the children of the late Richard T. Crane, the iron master, and is wealthy according to the highest American standards; but she does not consider that she has earned her wealth, and therefore devotes a large share of it to efforts to establish social conditions under which she and others of her class will not receive what they do not earn. Mrs. Gartz is not a Communist, but like myself, a member of the Socialist party, compelled to advertise Communists by the stupid persecutions to which they are subjected.

It is the custom of Mrs. Gartz to write what she calls "letters of protest" to those in high places; four bound volumes of these letters are read by radicals in all parts of the world. Reading in the paper that the jury had brought in a verdict of guilty, Mrs. Gartz thought that the case was settled, so she wrote to Judge Allison. Here is the letter:

JUDGE CHARLES ALLISON
SAN BERNARDINO, CALIF.

DEAR SIR:
IT WAS A GREAT SURPRISE TO BELIEVERS IN JUSTICE that the Young Communists were found guilty in your court. For some unknown reason many people, presumably intelligent, are afraid of ideas. In this case the idea is that the Red Flag means danger, but danger to what? There is danger only to the conservative idea that the world in which we live is perfect as it is. The people who take the Red Flag as their emblem feel that there is plenty of room for improvement, and I for one do not blame them, because I realize the many shortcomings of the present order of society all over the world. Man's

inhumanity to man is the biggest factor in this manmade world, which the youth of the world is rising against in every country. They ought to be encouraged instead of clapped into jail. Couldn't you tell, as you listened to "Yetta," that she was a young woman of high principles and ideals, and not a criminal fit only for crucifixion? Yes, we must listen to these young crusaders, and learn that there is a big work to be done in this world before we can rest on our oars and say, It is finished.

We would like to have more respect for our courts—would like to feel that they are unprejudiced, especially against the foreigner, who has long been invited to this country, with the hope of finding an earthly paradise. When he does not, and tries to better his condition, and that of all workers, he is considered a menace, and told to go back where he came from. Our only answer to unjust treatment is always a guilty one, because we do not know how to cope with the evils of our present social system. So, I say, go easy with these young enthusiasts.

KATE CRANE-GARTZ

For the writing of the above Mrs. Gartz was cited for contempt of court, and a crowded court room watched a somewhat unusual scene. Judge Allison inquired as to her purpose in writing the letter, and Mrs. Gartz explained with quiet dignity that she does not believe in sending people to an evil place like San Quentin for any cause, and least of all for the holding of unpopular opinions. She does not believe that these young people committed a felony, and considers that any citizen has a right to protest against cruel sentences being imposed for crimes of opinion. Judge Allison sternly informed her that at the time he received the letter the case was still before him, and if anyone could write a "private letter" to a judge, advising him what to do about a case, there could no longer be respect for our courts.

The remark about "a private letter" seemed somewhat of a joke, since, at the time the letter was mailed to the judge, a copy had been sent to "The Open Forum," the little paper of our Civil Liberties

Union, which reaches a couple of thousand people in Southern California. The letter was published in "The Open Forum" October 19th, four days before Judge Allison was due to sentence the prisoners. But perhaps it was just as well that Mrs. Gartz and her attorney did not mention this publication to the judge! He fined her seventy-five dollars. She wished to appeal, but was informed that under California law the only basis of appeal could be that the judge had no jurisdiction—which he obviously had in this case.

I am interested to note this morning's newspapers dealing with the procedure according to their usual custom. The *Times* reports Mrs. Gartz as "modestly attired and wearing many diamonds." She wore a ring with one diamond, which she always wears. The *Examiner* reports that "she did not speak with the Los Angeles Communists while in court and took no part in the demonstration, that included much embracing and kissing, after the court pronounced judgment."

As a matter of fact she paid the cost of their bail-bonds, and invited them and their friends to a dinner-party at the very swankyest hotel in the whole area, which I won't name, as it is well enough advertised anyhow. When the party of nineteen reached the place we found the open-air dining room in the very fancy patio half filled by a banquet of the County Committee of the Republican party. The wealth and fashion of the region, the very same patriotic kind that was sending the Communists to jail! You could not have told it from a similar banquet in New York: the gentlemen just as rosy and well-groomed, and the ladies in their chiffon and satin tails, the latest fashion from Paris.

A sumptuous affair and an edifying experience for five working-class felons out on bail! They had been eating beans and potatoes at their two meals per day in the county jail; now they ate toasted marrow and hors d'oeuvres, and ripe olives and celery, and consomme en tasse, and filet of sole a la I forget what, and lemon sherbet, and roast young turkey with dressing, and October spring lamb, and hearts of lettuce with mayonnaise, and peach shortcake and ice cream, and demi tasse and cheese and crackers—we began to weaken, and few of us got to the end of the menu. The liberal ladies of our party lit their cigarettes, and so did many of the Republican committee ladies, but I was interested to note that all five of the convicted felons declined to smoke. I noticed also that a chorus off stage serenaded us during the repast, and the first song was

> My country, 'tis of thee,
> Sweet land of liberty—

which speaks well for the patriotism of the Republican leaders of the orange belt, but not so well for their sense of humor!

I forgot to add that I was introduced to Judge Allison. He was cordial, and kind enough to say that he was pleased. I replied: "Now that the matter is over, I suppose it is all right for me to point out to you that California has again acquired some political prisoners, which is very bad for its reputation with the rest of the world." The Judge replied that he had not been able to help what had happened; it was the legislature which enacted the law, and the jury which decided the question of guilt. This you will recognize as what Pontius Pilate said in the case of another political prisoner.

I said to the Judge: "I suppose that you and I, as citizens, now-have a right to urge the repeal of this red flag law." He replied: "We certainly have." I said: "I shall take pleasure in coming to you before long with a petition to the legislature for its repeal." He did not say that he would sign it, but he did convey to me the fact that he was a Democrat in politics. I was too polite to tell him that the bones of Thomas Jefferson would rise up in their grave to denounce a "Democrat" judge who enforced alien and sedition laws of the kind which Jefferson had made the chief object of his antagonism. I here remind Judge Allison of Jefferson's saying to the effect that mankind has nothing to fear from error, provided that reason is left free to combat it. Also of his sterner saying which reads: "The tree of liberty must be refreshed from time to time with the blood of patriots and tyrants. It is its natural."

Three

"We Will Make Our Own Pictures": Creating Popular Culture

When I have an impulse to quarrel with any kind of a comrade, I sublimate it by quarreling with the capitalists.
—*Upton Sinclair to Mike Gold, October 25, 1928*

UPTON SINCLAIR HAD A complicated relationship with the movie industry. He was fascinated with the potential of motion pictures, and actors Charlie Chaplin and Douglas Fairbanks were among his closest friends. Sinclair scholar John Ahouse has speculated that although Sinclair wrote exposés of "the pulpit, the lectern, or the editor's desk" in the twenties, he did not write a similar exposé of Hollywood in that period, perhaps because he hoped to still influence the industry.[1] Following his film version of *The Jungle*, he wrote "The Adventurer," which was produced in 1917 as a silent film by the U.S. Amusement Corporation. His 1908 novel *The Moneychangers* was produced by Federal Photoplays in 1920, but Sinclair found it unrecognizable. His 1922 novel *They Call Me Carpenter* opens with World War I veterans rioting against the showing of the German film *The Cabinet of Doctor Caligari*.

In the first two decades of the twentieth century, movies were far more self-consciously political and varied in their ideologies. Since film production was relatively inexpensive (between $400 and $1,000 per film), radicals, reformers, and women's groups, as well as

ALL STAR FEATURE CORP. presents IN MOTION PICTURES
- UPTON SINCLAIR'S -
WONDERFUL STORY OF THE BEEF PACKING INDUSTRY
THE JUNGLE
FEATURING
GEORGE NASH
GAIL KANE
AND THE AUTHOR
5 DARING ACTS
210 ASTOUNDING SCENES

"IT'S THE MEAT THAT MADE HER SICK"

When *The Jungle* was screened in 1921, J. D. Cannon, the founder of the Labor Film Service, wrote to Sinclair that "the picture ended with the audience spontaneously coming to its feet, cheering enthusiastically and tumultuously."

conservative organizations, could produce films to present their causes to the public.[2] Steven Ross estimates that between 1905 and 1917, 46 percent of films were liberal, 34 percent were conservative, 7 percent were populist, and 4 percent were radical.[3] But by the twenties, filmmaking was less an art form than a multimillion dollar industry with close ties to Wall Street.

Although Sinclair excoriated the "script-writing mills" in *The Golden Scenario,* a novella written during the Depression, he also fervently believed in the power of popular culture to educate the public and was gratified when two of his books were made into films. *The Wet Parade* (1931) and *The Gnome-mobile* (1962) took his messages of temperance and ecology to new audiences.

Sinclair also financed a groundbreaking film shot in Mexico by the brilliant Russian filmmaker Sergei Eisenstein. Paramount Studios had brought Eisenstein to Hollywood in 1930 to study the new techniques of using sound in motion pictures. Four months after his arrival, his contract was terminated due to his notoriety as a Soviet filmmaker. When Eisenstein decided to make a film about Mexico, Charlie Chaplin persuaded Sinclair to finance the project. Sinclair, who had been fascinated by Eisenstein's *Potemkin,* wrote to him that "a great artist [was to be] permitted to make one picture the way he wanted it," and then invested $25,000 in the film.[4] He sent his wife's brother, Hunter Kimbrough, to Mexico as a chaperone to the unruly Eisenstein. A combination of drunken brawls in Mexico, pornographic drawings sent from Eisenstein to the Sinclairs, and finally, Mary Craig Sinclair's outrage when their home was refinanced to send additional funding, doomed the project.[5] Sinclair insisted that Eisenstein hand over his unfinished footage before returning to Russia and gave it to film editor Sol Lesser.

Sinclair arranged a release of the film as *Thunder over Mexico* in a condensed, one-hour version in New York in 1933. In 1951, he attempted to release the full footage but was thwarted by the prejudices of the McCarthy era. The three-hour film was stored in a vault from 1951 to 1954 and was finally donated to the Museum of Modern Art by Bud Lesser. Film curator Eileen Bowser wrote to Bud Lesser, "The film is very much alive in its various forms...we regard it as one of our greatest treasures."[6]

In 1933, Sinclair's self-published novel *Upton Sinclair Presents William Fox* (founder of Fox Film, the progenitor of Twentieth Century–Fox) documented the war between the independent producer and the corporate financiers of motion pictures, using chapter titles like "The Vultures" and "The Octopus." Sinclair commented,

"No melodrama that I have been able to invent had been more packed with crimes and betrayals, perils and escapes, than the story of William Fox."[7] Fox employees were forbidden to read the book, and John Ahouse comments that "the Fox book, together with his involvement in the Sergei Eisenstein production fiasco the previous year, guaranteed animosity from the film community when Sinclair opened his campaign for governor only a few months later."[8] His exposure of reactionary politics within the studios led to a fierce attack during his gubernatorial campaign, including the industry's first use of faked newsreels in electoral politics.[9]

Notes:

1. John Ahouse, "Upton Sinclair's Hollywood," in Lionel Rolfe, *Literary L.A.* (Los Angeles: California Classics, 2002)

2. Steven J. Ross, "How Hollywood Became Hollywood," in *Metropolis in the Making*, ed. Tom Sitton and William Deverell (Berkeley: University of California Press, 2001), 255

3. Ibid., 297-298

4. Harry Geduld and Ron Gottesman, *Sergei Eisenstein and Upton Sinclair: The Making and Unmaking of* Que Viva Mexico! (Bloomington: University of Indiana, 1970)

5. "It was the greatest blunder we ever made," Mary Craig wrote in *Southern Belle* (New York: Crown Publishers, 1957), 331.

6. Correspondence from Bowser to Bud Lesser cited in Lesser's "The Rescue of Que Viva Mexico!" in *Upton Sinclair Quarterly* 12:1-2, Fall 1988, 4-26

7. Upton Sinclair, *Upton Sinclair Presents William Fox* (Los Angeles: Upton Sinclair, 1933), ix

8. John Ahouse, *Upton Sinclair: A Descriptive, Annotated Bibliography* (Los Angeles: Arundel Press, 1994), 7

9. See Greg Mitchell, *The Campaign of the Century* (New York: Random House, 1992)

Big Business and Its Movies
from *Screenland* magazine, 1922

EVEN IN THE relatively open first decades of moviemaking, radical films drew fierce attack from elites. Nickelodeons, cheap halls where working-class immigrants could see films for a nickel, were the sites of tremendous controversy in this period, drawing opposition for the progressive films they often showed. In 1911, when *Capital vs. Labor* was filmed, mounted police were called; they charged into the actors playing strikers, causing numerous injuries. *Locked Out*, with scenes of starvation in the homes of strikers, police beatings, and the ghosts of these martyrs confronting the owner of the factory, drew a complaint from *Motion Picture World*. The *World* complained that the National Board of Censorship should have rejected this film and that exhibitors should not "excite the masses by showing them innocent women killed in the act of earning their daily bread."[1]

On the other hand, anti-labor films were also so numerous that in 1910 the American Federation of Labor convention endorsed resolutions advising workers to protest to local management whenever these films were shown. The AFL convention urged the labor movement to begin the production of "motion pictures depicting the real life and ideals of the working class."[2] In 1914, trade union activist Elias Strunsky offered Sinclair financing to produce a film version of *The Jungle*, later described by historian Philip Foner as "the first full-length pro-labor film produced in the United States.[3] *The Kinematograph* and *Lantern Weekly* commented on its effectiveness: "After seeing the picture we begin to have burned into us that Packingtown made enormous profits not simply out of tainted food, but out of the ruined lives of men and women."[4] However, trade journals reported that pressure was coming from movie moguls to keep *The Jungle* out of motion picture houses beyond the big cities.[5] Sinclair himself loaned it to a political group and never got it back. "Whoever has it, please let me know," he wrote.[6] The picture has never been recovered.

Between 1916 and 1946, moviemaking became the biggest industry in California. Although Southern California's climate was ideal for filming, its main attraction for investors was the fact that open shop labor practices ensured cheap labor. By the 1920s, the scandalous conduct of stars in a series of risqué movies had prompted the industry to recruit former Postmaster General Will Hays from President Warren G. Harding's cabinet to become "movie czar," initiating the censorship that Sinclair chronicles in "Big Business and Its Movies." Such analyses of the ideological agenda of the film industry are uncommon today, but in the twenties they were part of popular culture: Sinclair's essay was published in Screenland, next to ads asking, "The Book of Fate: What Is Going to Happen to You?" and "Have You an Idea for a Movie Star?"

Notes

1. *Motion Picture World*, May 13, 1911, 1082; cited in Eileen Bowser, *The Transformation of Cinema* (New York: Charles Scribner Inc., 1990), 189

2. Philip Foner, "Upton Sinclair's 'The Jungle': The Movie" in Dieter Herms ed., *Upton Sinclair: Literature and Social Reform* (Frankfurt, Peter Lang, 1990), 150

3. Ibid., 151

4. November 26, 1914, 24

5. Film Corporation Records and Sinclair Manuscripts, Lilly Library, University of Indiana

6. Upton Sinclair, *The Autobiography of Upton Sinclair* (New York: Harcourt Brace and World, 1962), 204

———

THE MOVIES ARE MADE for children, and for grown people who have remained at the mental age of children; these constitute the bulk of our population, and anything which they could not understand, and particularly anything which would offend them, is automatically ruled out. So the movie world is a world of sticky sweet sentimentality, of rigid propriety, and of hard and fast conventionality. It is a fairy-tale world, full of infantile wish fulfillments, into which the harsh and painful facts of everyday life are never by any possibility permitted to break. Most people believe in this kind of world, and it is the kind which the director and the actor would portray if left to themselves.

Money Dictates Motion Pictures

But it is not the director and the actor who decide what goes into pictures. The final say rests with the producer, or his backer with the money, and these have their own ideas of what they wish the people to believe.

Let us take an illustration. All the vested interests of the entire world wish the people to believe that the present Russian government is a government of degenerates and criminals. So we have had a flood of anti-Russian propaganda pictures. Let us describe one of them—*The World and Its Women*, by Thompson Buchanan. The star in this case is Lou Tellegen, and he makes a magnificent young Russian nobleman. We are taken back to the days before the revolution, and we see the beautiful fairy-tale method applied to czarist Russia.

Flood of Anti-Russian Propaganda

The elegant young nobleman drives his prancing steeds and he so dearly loves his humble, adoring peasants and is so good and generous to them! Never, never do you see him laying the knout upon the backs of the peasants, never do you see the troops of the Czar driving them out into the wilderness to starve because their crops have failed, and they have not paid their taxes! Never does this noble young Russian waste his substance in gambling, or upon the brilliant kept women of St. Petersburg. No, the aristocracy has become a band of saints, and the only wicked people in Russia are the revolutionists. Those glorious heroes and martyrs, the men and women who gave their lives to deliver Russia from the hideous yoke of the Czar— these have become a gang of bomb-throwing conspirators with twisted, degenerate faces and the vilest personal vices!

Then comes the revolution; and these wicked ruffians begin to murder and torture the beautiful and noble Russian aristocrats. You will not need me to tell you what comes next. No propaganda of world capitalism against Soviet Russia would be complete without the nationalization of women! In this case, of course, it is a pure and beautiful American girl who is to be "nationalized"; and, of course, it is the handsome and noble young Russian aristocrat who rescues her; and, of course, it is warships flying Old Glory which achieve the final deliverance. It is a tradition of Broadway and 42nd Street that whenever George M. Cohan found he had a bum show, he would save it by rushing on the stage waving two American flags.

Is This Deliberate Class Lying?

This kind of deliberate class lying now constitutes practically all of what feeble intellectual life our moving pictures possess. Some years ago I had the pleasure of talking with Mr. D. W. Griffith and voiced my abhorrence of the incitement to race hatred which makes the essence of his picture *The Birth of a Nation*. His answer was that he had not been thinking about that aspect of the matter; he had merely been concerned to tell an effective story, and had not cared what it was about.

But since that time the movies have come to full consciousness; they have now a Big Business director, at a salary of a hundred and fifty thousand dollars a year, and they have gone on a huge scale into the business of protecting organized greed by making it holy to the people of America—I understand that Mr. Griffith is now completing a mammoth picture, intended to preach what is called patriotism—that is to say, capitalist imperialism.

Mr. Griffith's Next Picture

American financiers are forcing their loans upon China, and all the states of Central and South America; and when these loans are not met, American battleships and American marines are to be used to collect the debts, and the moving pictures are to be used to keep the people in a frenzy of delight over this "patriotic" course of action. Mr. Griffith has now had the backing of Mr. Hays; he has had the free use of the American army and navy. We may be sure that this time he won't pretend to anybody that he was just interested in telling a story; this time he will be a real and devoted patriot.

And if the producers should not be strenuous enough in protecting the exploiters in their rights to what the rest of us produce by our toil, why then there comes the censor to teach them better. Ten years ago I assisted in the production of one fairly honest moving picture—that is, one which tried to follow out at least a few of the author's ideas. The picture was *The Jungle* and it is interesting to note that the concern which made it was forced into bankruptcy almost before the picture was shown.

Tried to Make Films for Masses
Three or four years ago all effort was made to organize a company to make and distribute pictures in the interest of the workers. This company tried to show *The Jungle* to make a little money and get a start; and all over the country they ran into the censor. The picture was barred from Chicago absolutely, and the secretary of the censorship board made no bones about the reason; the picture was an attack upon Chicago's biggest and most powerful industry. Then came the National Board of Review, ordering the removal of a caption describing the United States of America as "Not just the sweet land of liberty." Also they ordered the removal of a caption in a court scene, "Pleading for Justice." This seemed to convey the idea that workingmen sometimes did not get justice in the United States without pleading for it! I should like to get this movie censor to read a book called "Justice and the Poor," which tells the facts on this subject—and tells them without the endorsement of Chief Justice Taft of the U.S. Supreme Court!

The Wet Parade
1931–1932

LIKE THE PROTAGONISTS of his novel *The Wet Parade*, Upton Sinclair grew up hating liquor and its destructiveness. Such individuals rarely end up as the main characters in films; more often, they are simply the victims of a fascinating and self-destructive main character. Sinclair chose to construct a different narrative; he wanted to remind the country that the Prohibition movement originated in the tragedies of families of alcoholics.

Sinclair's temperance beliefs were expressed most passionately in *The Wet Parade* (1931) and the film based on it (1932). He was inspired to write *The Wet Parade* when he saw a poll by *Literary Digest* suggesting that the public was ready to repeal Prohibition.[1] He initially tried to arrange a filmed debate with an actor playing him against a Clarence Darrow–like opponent. When this plan fell through, he wrote *The Wet Parade*.

Irving Thalberg bought *The Wet Parade* for $25,000 but subsequently barred Sinclair from his MGM lot because of his politics.[2] When the film premiered at Grauman's Chinese Theater in March 1932, the audience called for Sinclair to speak, but Sid Grauman prevented it, ostensibly on the grounds that Sinclair was not wearing a tuxedo.[3] Sinclair then arranged a debate on Prohibition between *Wet Parade* star Walter Huston (who portrayed the alcoholic father but argued against Prohibition in the debate) and the evangelist Aimee Semple McPherson (who argued for Prohibition but, ironically, later worked against Sinclair's gubernatorial candidacy).

The Wet Parade was disconcerting to viewers because it brought a distinctly political tone into the debate about alcohol, clearly demonstrating how economic and political interests were served by the distribution of liquor during Prohibition. One film reviewer commented: "It is a record for the nation's archive...more than Hollywood entertainment, a grim indictment of our time spread with bitter laughter. It makes people think."[4]

Addiction researcher Robin Room, who assembled a four-night series on "Alcohol Images in American Film" at the Pacific Film Archive in 1982, commented: "I found *The Wet Parade* really fascinating; more of it stuck in my mind than from any other film in the whole series."[5] In the program notes, Room wrote:

> What is most striking about *The Wet Parade* to the modern viewer is the degree to which alcohol is a political matter...[the film's] ambivalence is a poignant reflection of its historical location at a point of inflection between two frames of cultural consciousness.[6]

Notes

1. Leon Harris, *Upton Sinclair: American Rebel* (New York: Thomas Crowell, 1975), 267

2. Two years later, Irving Thalberg would be a major player in defeating Sinclair's campaign for governor of California.

3. Greg Mitchell, *The Campaign of the Century* (New York: Random House, 1992), 303-304

4. Regina Crewe, *The American*, April 24, 1932

5. Personal correspondence, Room to Coodley, November 8, 1996

6. Pacific Film Archive program notes, February 9, 1982

THE GOLDEN MOON climbed higher, and turned to silver. The radio howled and made noises like a frying-pan on a hot stove, and now and then a fragment of music or a voice: "Good evening, friends of radioland!" A breeze sprang up from over the water, and Kip got Maggie May's wrap for her, and they sat discussing the state of their hearts, and the strange bewilderment that had afflicted them. Now that it was over, Maggie May said it had been silly of them not to find out long ago; but Kip said, how could he have dreamed that Maggie May would think of marrying such an uninteresting person as himself—and when there were so many brilliant and entertaining men all around her. Why had she ever turned them down? She thought it over, and replied: "I used to watch them, and try to make up my mind—because of course Cousin Jenny kept telling me their good points. One thing, I waited to see one of them refuse a drink of liquor, and I didn't see it."

"You wouldn't marry a man that drinks even a little bit, Maggie May?"

"Would you expect me to, with the experiences I've had?" Later on, when Kip told this to Jerry Tyler, the bright young man of Manhattan chuckled gaily, and sang an old refrain, to the effect that "The lips that touch liquor shall never touch mine!" A song which had inspired our grandmothers, he said; but Maggie May had never heard it.

Kip asked his future wife, with no little curiosity, what it was she had in mind as an occupation, in case her husband continued to be a failure as a money-maker. At first Maggie May wouldn't tell him; she said he would laugh at her—and sure enough he did, serious-minded young man though he was. Such an odd notion for a girl to take up! Maggie May said she would like to be a temperance lecturer!

She told him how this idea had come to her. Walking one afternoon through a cross-street in New York, on her way to keep an engagement with her cousin, she had come upon a church, of some evangelical sort, with a sign in front saying that a man was giving a temperance lecture inside. Being early for her engagement, she had gone in to hear what it was like; and so the idea had taken root.

"You liked it so well?" asked Kip.

"I liked it so little," she replied. "There was a feeble old man, and fifteen or twenty old women. He talked about the Bible and the love of God, which doesn't mean much to people nowadays. Then he talked about the Constitution, and reverence for law—and we can see how that counts. People want what they want, and the law be hanged."

"So you wanted to improve the lecture?"

"A girl doesn't have the sort of experiences I've had without being made to think. For ten years or so I watched my father; and now there's an uncle down home, and several friends of the family. Up here there's Roger, and Evelyn, and Dick. So I keep asking

The film version of Sinclair's novel *The Wet Parade* was released in 1932. As the feminist son of an alcoholic, Sinclair strove to bring national attention to the reasons for the Eighteenth Amendment

Who's Who in "The Wet Parade"

Robert Young as
Kip Tarleton

Kip was old Pow Tarleton's boy . . . world tried to lick him and couldn't—you'll be glad to meet him—how he did love that Maggie May girl—fought for her —defied friends and family to hold her. . . .

They called her "Persimmon" —robbed of her childhood—a woman before she was a girl because of the selfishness of man— she did love Kip and that made up for everything. . . .

Dorothy Jordan as
Maggie May

Lewis Stone as
Roger Chilcote, Sr.

Down in Louisiana everyone knew Papa Chilcote—proud remnant of old southern aristocracy —with gray goatee and broad-brimmed hat—drink—yes—deplored Republicanism—and seltzer in his bourbon — had too many friends, and only one enemy.

Poor Man's Club—that's what Pow Tarleton called the corner saloon—Pow was quite a clubman—everybody liked him—a power on Wall Street . . . they said drink got him—but he was an enemy of prohibition to the end.

Walter Huston as
Pow Tarleton

Jimmy Durante as
Abe Shilling

Here's Abe—good old Abe Shilling of the prohibition service . . . body of a gladiator . . . face of a gnu . . . embittered by the fact every outstretched hand held a herring—you will split your sides following him on his rounds of the New York speakeasies. . . .

They still talk about Roger, Jr., in Chilcote and on Broadway —he learned about women from Eileen Pinchon and it was a liberal education—started each day with a new suit and a hangover— chip off the old block—inherited father's pride—and weakness.

Neil Hamilton as
Roger Chilcote

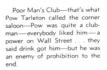

myself: Why do people drink? And what can you say to them? What's the right way to go at it?"

"What *is* the right way?"

"The first thing is to begin when they're young. It's no good talking to grown people. If they're not drinkers, they don't need it, and if they are drinkers they laugh at you."

"Aren't Evelyn and Dick young enough?"

"No, they should have been taught when they were children. Somebody ought to have said to them: Look, this is what drinking does to you."

"If I say that," said Kip, "people point out the ones it hasn't seemed to hurt. Each one thinks he'll escape."

"You see a dozen people drinking, and out of the dozen, one will die a drunkard. Maybe it'll be you, and maybe the next one. You throw dice with death."

"Yes, but people want to gamble. That's their idea of a good time."

"They wouldn't, if you could bring it home to them. You've got to say: This is the kind of fool you look like; this is the kind you talk like."

Said Kip: "I only know this New York bunch, of course. They don't care what they look like, and they know that no one is listening to the way they talk. You try to separate them from their booze, and they make you a subject for wise-cracks."

"Well, people like that have to go on till they've had enough. Sooner or later, you know, every drunkard wants to stop. My father couldn't, but he would warn others. I can hardly bring myself to think about him, and the things I went through, up to the very end; yet I believe I could stand on a platform and tell a group of school children everything about it. I'd say: This is what I saw, with my own eyes. This is what liquor did to my father. They'd be interested in that, don't you think?

Kip said, no longer smiling: "You tell them about your father, and I'll tell them about mine."

The Golden Scenario

1930s

IN THE CONSERVATIVE Republican climate of the 1920s, in which Hollywood was emerging as a corporate entity, studios tried to expand their audience base and increase profits by creating an experience of fantasy with a cross-class audience.[1] They built exotic picture palaces and produced lavish pictures designed to turn moviegoing into an experience that stressed individualism rather than collective action.[2] Sinclair explored early Hollywood in *The Golden Scenario*, written sometime during the Depression and unpublished until 1994.[3] Sinclair scholar John Ahouse describes it as a "riff on movie script mills and the studios' manipulation of story ideas, which were abuses he had experienced firsthand."[4]

After the success of the film *The Wet Parade* in 1932, Irving Thalberg had invited Sinclair to write another screenplay, about the contrasting lives of the rich and the poor. Sinclair received $10,000 for a first draft of what he called "The Gold Spangled Banner" but never heard about it again. In the late thirties, Sinclair commented that all of his screenplays had been rejected for indicting the profit system. *Oil!*, he wrote, "has been read by every concern in the business, and never have they reported but one thing: 'magnificent, but dangerous.'"[5] Perhaps his bitterness with the industry is reflected in *The Golden Scenario*, a novella reminiscent of Harry Leon Wilson's *Merton of the Movies* and foreshadowing Nathaneal West's *The Day of the Locust*, documenting the rot inside the Hollywood apple.[6]

It would be three decades after *The Wet Parade* before another Sinclair book was made into a film. John Ahouse comments: "An author not generally known for his whimsy, Sinclair nevertheless indulged himself from time to time in satiric or playful ideas such as *The Spokesman's Secretary* from 1926, *The Gnomobile* from 1936, or *Our Lady* from 1938, stories at the farthest remove from the gritty

When Sinclair finished writing *The Gnomobile*, a mutual friend introduced
him to Walt Disney, suggesting the book could be made into a children's
film. Disney responded that the story wasn't right for cartoon characters, but
that if he ever switched to live actors, he would do it.

reality of the Chicago stockyards, or the anarchy trials in Boston."[7]
At the end of the EPIC campaign in 1934, Sinclair left Los Angeles
by car to raise funds to pay off his campaign debts. As he told Ron
Gottesman:

> I drove through the redwood forest. I'd never seen it before. And it was
> miraculous to me, the marvelous trees—one of them so big that they've
> cut a hole through the trunk for the automobiles to drive through. And
> the ground was completely covered with a great mass of ferns. And I

imagined little gnomes living in those ferns. Because I always think of stories, you see, I had the idea of a little girl wandering among those ferns.[8]

The *Gnomobile* may well have been the first children's adventure story with a moral about saving the environment.[9] When it was published in 1936, Sinclair's friend Rob Wagner, publisher of *Script* magazine, took him to see Walt Disney, suggesting it would make a good movie. Disney explained that the story wasn't right for cartoon characters, but if they ever switched to live actors, he would do it. Sinclair later explained:

> Well, he began using live characters so I wrote and reminded him of his promise, and I didn't hear from him, but every once in a while I would write and remind him....And lo and behold, a few months ago, he wrote me that all right, he would keep his promise....I don't know just when he will do it, but I hope to live to see *The Gnomobile* as a movie.[10]

The Gnome-mobile was released in 1965, three years before Sinclair's death.[11]

Notes

1. Steven J. Ross, "How Hollywood Became Hollywood," in *Metropolis in the Making*, ed. Tom Sitton and William Deverill (Berkeley: University of California Press, 2001), 257

2. Ibid., 266

3. It was published in *Los Angeles Magazine* 39:12, December 1994.

4. John Ahouse, "Upton Sinclair's Hollywood," in Lionel Rolfe, *Literary L.A.* (Los Angeles: California Classics, 2002), adapted for presentation at American Literary Association conference, Cambridge, Mass., 2003

5. Upton Sinclair, "The Movies and Political Propoganda" in William J. Perlman, ed., *The Movies on Trial* (New York: Macmillan, 1936)

6. John Ahouse writes: "Wilson's serialized novel follows its title character from his hometown in Illinois, where he spends all his time watching the moving pictures, to his quest for being in them. This takes him to early Hollywood...Like the legions of hopefuls who still arrive in this town every day, he has a lot to learn." Personal correspondence to Coodley, May 15, 2004.

   West took many of the settings and minor characters of his novel directly from his experience living in a hotel on Hollywood Boulevard. *The Day of the Locust* is regarded as West's masterpiece and still stands as one of the best novels written about the early years of Hollywood.

7. Ahouse, "Upton Sinclair's Hollywood" ALA talk

8. Ron Gottesman, Interview with Upton Sinclair, Columbia Oral History Project, 311. The drive to preserve the redwoods had begun in 1918, after John Merriam, Madison Grant, and Henry Fairfield Osborn had viewed the widespread destruction of the forest along the newly made Highway 101 in Humboldt County and organized the Save the Redwoods League.

9. Many children's books by then were lyrical celebrations of nature; for example, see L. M. Montgomery's 1908 *Anne of Green Gables*. But "more than any of the other topics dealt with in the literature for children, the treatment of environmental problems is inadequate...few offer any alternatives or solutions." (Patricia Cianciolo, *Adventuring with Books* (Urbana, Ill.: National Council of Teachers of English, 1977), 7

10. Gottesman/Sinclair Interview, 312

11. Jack Zipes argues in *Happily Ever After: Fairy Tales, Children and the Culture Industry* (New York: Routledge, 1998) that Disney, as the predominant purveyor of fairy tales, is a major force in socializing children to consumer culture. Zipes concludes that fairy tales must be recaptured by storytellers to create community values that will combat the market culture.

D ANNY DANE WAS a true child of the movies; his mother having been a fan before him, and having named him in anticipation of his future career. In 1930, at the age of seventeen, he was flourishing, with a brick-red complexion, very auburn hair, shining blue eyes and a naive, eager expression. He was a child of hope, of faith, of trust in the moral forces which guide the universe.

Danny was the nephew of the proprietress in Mother Carey's boardinghouse in Johannesburg, Missouri. She had no children of her own, but had raised Danny from babyhood, and he was her reason for slaving until her knuckles grew big and hard. The Depression might reduce the diets of the other boarders, but Danny had a glass of milk before he went to bed and picked up something in the kitchen when he came home from school.

Like most children of the movie era, Danny had passed through various cultural stages. At the outset, of course, he had worshiped at the shrines of the boy-gods; living the wholesome outdoor life of

Zane Grey, galloping over the wide-open spaces upon the glorious black charger of Tom Mix. Danny had been so many different sheriffs and had fought so many two-gun battles, and lassoed so many desperadoes and dragged them through the dust, that his mind had become a blur. But one lesson had been indelibly graven into it— that a lovely and pure-minded heroine waited for him at the end of the trail, with every blond hair of her head perfectly marcelled, no matter how roughly she had been handled by the desperate band of horse thieves at her father's Bar-X ranch.

From that stage Danny had become a monotheist, like his aunt, Anna Carey, worshiping at the altar of the Great God Douglas Fairbanks. He had hunted the wild deer in Sherwood Forest, making mock of the mighty sheriff of Nottingham; he had engaged in breathtaking swordplay with D'Artagnan, and had made his prisoners walk the plank with the Black Pirate.

The Clark Gable fan among the boarders was Miss Turlock, who ran the beauty parlor. Mr. Wink, floorwalker at Zellerman's department store, had begun his career at the Emporium in Kansas City, and thus affected the cosmopolitan point of view. His taste in movies was decidedly worldly, and although he was a frail little man, he made truly impish remarks about the ample curves of Mae West, and the heavings of the bosom of Gloria Swanson.

Professor Henniger, the "star" boarder, taught mathematics and philosophy at Union High School. He said he went to the movies in order to help the children select the right kind. Just now he was loud in the praises of *Little Women*, and he had recently written a letter to Miss Pickford, begging her to return to the screen.

There was only one theater in Johannesburg, the Rialto, and its programs changed every night, so by means of the double bill, the people had fourteen cultural opportunities every week. The patrons of Mother Carey's boardinghouse were seldom able to take in all these, even at the 14-cent price; but somebody always went when there was a really important star, and so at breakfast, lunch, and supper the next day there was enlightening conversation. The lucky guest told just how the hero and heroine conducted themselves at the crucial moments, after which general discussion broke out.

And then, of course, there were the "fan" magazines. These were expensive, and the advantage lay with Miss Pansy Betts, who was employed in the Globe drugstore, having access to a spread of riches all day. She knew what stars ate, and what they wore, what cars they drove—above all, what salaries they received. Danny Dane listened to the boarders, and when he was forbidden to attend a certain show, he read detailed accounts of it in *Screen Bits* or *Film Wonders*, freely loaned about in the establishment. So matters stood on the day when the Golden Scenario first cast its spell over Mother Carey's.

You know, of course, that among the dreams which haunt the souls of film fans—next to the one of going to Hollywood and earning five times as much as the President of the United States—is the dream of writing a scenario and having it accepted and produced. Every now and then one of Mother Carey's boarders would announce that he or she had a new idea for a scenario. This pregnant one would become secretive, and withdrawn from normal social life, and take to filling sheets of brown wrapping paper with penciled writing. The composition would be mailed to Paramount or Universal, and either it would come back with a printed rejection slip, or else be lost forever.

But hope springs eternal in the movie breast. It was Miss Pansy Betts who started the excitement about the Golden Scenario. She brought in at lunchtime a copy of *Talkie Topics*, and entrusted it to Professor Henniger, she herself not being sure of the long words. He read aloud an advertisement, as follows:

"DO YOU WANT FAME AND FORTUNE? These may be yours if you have the idea we need. We are seeking the great motion-picture story of next year. Have you got it? Maybe you have—you never know till you try. THE GOLDEN SCENARIO, we are calling it. Send us your ideas, and a committee of competent judges will read your script. If we find the BIG IDEA we are looking for, we will pay you one thousand dollars cash, AND IN ADDITION one half of whatever the studio pays us for the scenario. Do you know that Theodore Dreiser received NINETY THOUSAND DOLLARS for the screen rights of his novel *An American Tragedy?* We are close to the scene, and can represent your interests. It costs you nothing to enter this contest. Write your outline the best you can, and mail it to NATIONAL SCREEN WRITERS AGENCY, DRAWER 4F, BOX 1167, HOLLYWOOD, CALIFORNIA."

The boarders fell to discussing the Golden Scenario—a marvelous title. They saw it shining before their eyes, they heard it jingling in their pockets, and excited discussion broke out at the table. What *would* be the theme of next year's winner? Professor Henniger was sure it would be a sweet domestic story—*Little Women* and *The Little Minister* proved the movies had discovered the soul. Mr. Wink scoffed at this idea, declaring all men in America were waiting for a new *Red-Headed Woman.*

Danny was one of those who took fire from the talk about the Golden Scenario. What he wanted, with all his heart and soul, was to get to Hollywood. There was the center of all excitements, and anytime that he sat and thought for five minutes, that was where his thoughts took him. If he could get to Hollywood, things would begin to happen, and he would have something to write about.

THAT NIGHT, WHEN Danny's aunt sent him off to bed, he lay still, turning his problems over and over in his mind. The more he studied it, the more he became fixed in one conclusion—he must go to Hollywood and write the Golden Scenario, and bring the money back to his good kind aunt and all the boarders.

At last he dozed; and what it was that awakened him he never knew. Perhaps it was the whistle of the midnight freight, which passed only a couple of blocks from his bedroom window, and always stopped because there was a water tank, and a car or two to be picked up, with much backing and switching and bumping of cars together. Or perhaps it was the inspiration; the marvelous birth of an idea which took place in his sleep and suddenly was there, all fully formed like Venus made of sea foam—only they had never shown that in the movies, so Danny didn't know about it.

The idea was this: Mother Carey's had suddenly become interesting! This boardinghouse was to be put up on the screen, all those hard-pressed small-town people with their hopes and their fears; and then himself, Danny Dane, with such a nice name already made for the screen—Danny going to Hollywood and becoming the means of everybody's deliverance! Whatever happened to him in Hollywood—that would be the Golden Scenario! He would write it and find somebody to produce it, and perhaps he would act in it—anyhow, in one way or another he would make a fortune, and bring it back to Johannesburg, and that would be the happy ending!

Danny got out of bed, softly because old Mr. Givers, the Spanish War veteran, slept in the other half of the attic, with only a thin partition between. Danny slipped into his clothes—all but his shoes. He got himself a change of underwear, and a couple of clean shirts, and some handkerchiefs and socks, his new safety razor and a mail-order book entitled *How to Write for the Screen*. And last of all, a little clay "bank" into which his aunt had obliged him to drop a dime whenever he took old Mrs. Hooper for a drive. There were several dollars in it now, and it would be enough to buy food on the way to the city of his dreams.

With his shoes in one hand and his bundle in the other he tiptoed out of the room, and down two flights of creaky stairs, and through the kitchen and the back door. He heard a crashing of the freight cars—it might be the end of a shunting job—and once on the street Danny ran as hard as he could. He was just in time, for the long train had started its westward journey, and he had to take a leap to catch the iron ladder of a "gondola" as it swept by.

The first thing that happened to Danny Dane was that he stumbled over a body and was greeted with a volley of curses. So he realized that he was not the only young man who was going West by the agency of the "side-door Pullman." He stood motionless until his eyes made out the sleeping form in the darkness, and then he found vacant space and lay down. The next thing he did was to take the little clay jug out of his pocket and break it—the rattling of the train drowned the noise—and he collected the dimes and wrapped them in an inside pocket. He put his bundle under his head for a pillow, and wrapped one arm around it for greater safety.

When the companions of his journey offered to show him how to "mooch" food, he got off the train with them, but as quickly as possible he lost them, and bought crackers and cheese in a grocery, ate them quickly and "hopped" the next westbound freight. By these wise methods he avoided the troubles which might have befallen a seventeen-year-old making his first venture on "the road"; after three days and four nights of travel, he stood in the doorway of an empty freight car in a "high fog" at dawn, and saw the long train rattling down El Cajon Pass into the inland plain of Southern California.

Before many hours he was looking at orange trees—whole groves of them in blossom, with ripe golden fruit, and an incredibly sweet odor; he saw lemon trees and grapefruit, and banana plants and date palms growing in the front yards of homes no more pretentious than the boardinghouse in which he had been raised. It was the greatest hour of Danny Dane's lifetime, the dream which had been haunting him as far back as he could remember. He clutched the side of the car, and had a hard time to keep the tears of delight from running down his cheeks. The train rolled on through the orange country, through one lovely town after another until, at one station, Danny Dane saw a sight which lifted his adventure into high gear.

A motion-picture company was at work! No less than three of the big two-eyed cameras and a sound truck, and a group of acting folk with brown greasepaint and black eyebrows and scarlet lips; a lovely lady star, seated in a canvas chair, and an elegant gentleman star in a similar chair. Danny, lifelong devotee, knew in an instant what it was; they were "on location," taking some kind of scene at a railroad depot. The instant the sight registered in his brain, he was down from the freight car without a word to anyone, and was part of the curious crowd watching the free show.

His was no idle curiosity, like that of the other bystanders. For Danny it was a professional matter; he was studying every detail of the makeup, costume, and conduct of this group, the first live movie people he had ever seen. To be near them, he had left his home and all that was dear to him. With the speed of a moving film, a whole series of impressions were registering themselves upon his brain—the material for the Golden Scenario!

The lady star was quite the loveliest spectacle the lad from Johannesburg had ever beheld. She was not much older than himself, with golden blond hair, brown-paint complexion, ripe full lips, and an expression of such tempting loveliness that Danny's heart thumped against his ribs. She was clad in a strange way for the platform of a railroad station: a fancy pale blue peignoir of Chinese silk, with a great golden dragon on it, and under that what appeared to be a lacy nightgown, openwork silk stockings, and high-heeled golden slippers with jewels on them. There was something just faintly familiar about this alluring creature. Surely he had seen her—but in what picture? It couldn't have been very long ago, because she was so young. But he cudgeled his memory in vain.

There came the whistle of a train; and evidently that was what the company was waiting for. Everybody started into nervous motion: The cameramen laid hold of their machines, the lady star stood up on her high heels, the gentleman took his overcoat on one arm and walking stick in hand, while a property boy picked up his suitcase. A long train came in, bound east from Los Angeles, and evidently there had been prearrangement with the railroad company, for the engineer placed the observation car right by the sound truck. The male star ascended to the rear platform, with the actors forming a group behind him. The microphone was wheeled close, swinging from a long rod, so it hung just over the heads of the speaking actors.

Everybody worked with lightning speed, having evidently rehearsed the scene carefully. The man on the sound truck called out, "Test," and the male star lifted his voice: "No, this is the last." "Okay," called the man on the truck, and then, "Shoot!" ordered the director—that magic word Danny Dane had read a hundred times in the fan magazines, but he now heard spoken for the first time.

The cameras began to grind, and the scene leaped into action. Down the length of the car the lady star came running, her pale blue robe floating behind, revealing hints of her curves. She was looking up into the windows of the car with anguish upon her lovely face. She came to the rear platform, and there she saw the man. "Reggy!" she cried. "Reggy!" And with outstretched arms and heartbreak in her tones: "No! No! What are you doing, dear? It's all a mistake." The man stood with a cold, proud look upon his face, and when he spoke, his voice was icy. "It is the end. I have had all I can stand." She caught the handrail, and sought to clamber up to him, calling, "Reggy! Reggy, my love!" But he answered, unmoved, "Compose yourself, woman. Don't make a spectacle in this public place." As the wheels began to grind, and Reggy stood with folded arms, gazing down at her with scorn, the lovely creature sank down upon the track, and bowed her golden head almost to the cinders, sobbing—until the train was distant and the director said, "Cut. Very good, darling." The lady star got up, brushed the cinders from the golden Chinese dragon, pushed back a strand of hair from her eyes, and said, "When do we eat?"

Danny was still devouring her with his eyes; and suddenly his heart gave a great leap. She was moving toward him! She was going to speak to him!

She did speak. "Haven't we met?"

Danny was so excited that he could hardly make a sound. He gulped once or twice, and said, "I don't know, Miss. I thought..."

"What is your name?"

He told her "Danny"; and suddenly a light broke upon her face. "You're Danny Dane!"

"Yes, ma'am."

"Danny Dane, from good old Jo'burg!"

"Yes, ma'am."

She put out her hand. "Look at me, kid. Don't you remember me?"

"I've seen you somewhere."

"At the boardinghouse? What did they call it?"

"Mother Carey's."

"Yes, that's it! Don't you remember the little girl, Sally?"

The light leaped to Danny's mind, and shone now in his face. "Little Sally Gug..." He was going to say "Gugglethwaite"; but the girl shot up a warning finger. "Sssh! Not a soul knows that name. I am Lily Lowe. Keep my secret from the publicity hounds."

"I'll keep it," whispered the awe-stricken boy.

"And you didn't know me!"

"I kept thinking I knew you. I thought I'd seen you in a picture."

"Maybe you did. But oh, Danny, now I've got one that's going to knock 'em cold! The new picture of Howard Anselm." Then, as Danny looked blank: "You never heard of Howard Anselm?"

"What is he?"

"He's the famous author. You'll learn about him," said Lily. "He's the hill-topper here right now, and he thinks I'm all right."

She was gazing into Danny's face, and happiness was dancing in her eyes. "Oh, kid! I'm so glad to see you. Somebody from home! You can't imagine how lonesome I've been in this dump."

"Dump?" Danny's face was more than ever a blank. He thought she must mean this orange town where they had just shot a scene. But she cried: "Hollywood! Wait till you know it. It's a place where you can't have a pal. You'll see what I mean." She took him by the arm. "We'll get a bite to eat, and talk it over. Maybe I can get Howard to give you a part in the new picture."

"Oh, could you?" Danny's whole soul went into that cry; and the girl laughed.

"You poor boob. Come on, kid," said his old friend. "Come and meet the company." She led him down the street, following the other actors, who were heading for a hotel in which there was a restaurant. "You shall see how godlike they are, and what sublime things they carry in their heads."

Halfway to the hotel was a shiny new automobile standing by the curb; and by the automobile was some sort of foreign-looking man in a chauffeur's uniform. He saluted as Lily approached; she stopped and began staring at him intently. Suddenly she cried, "You've been at it again!"

"No, Miss Lowe!" he protested.

"Come here!" she commanded; and when he hesitated, she stamped her foot, as if to a disobedient dog: "Come here, I say!"

He came to her. "Closer!" and then: "Now, breathe!"

Suddenly she raised her hand and put the palm of it into his face, and shoved him fiercely away. "I'm through with you!" she stormed. "If you think you're going to get arrested again with me in the car, you've missed your guess. Dirty booze hound!"

She turned to Danny. "Kid, do you know how to drive a car?"

"Yes—er—Lily—"

"And do you ever get drunk while you're driving?"

"I never drink."

"And you want a job?"

"Of course!"

"All right then, you're my chauffeur." She stepped up to the other man, and jerked the cap from his head, and went over and slapped it onto Danny's head. "That's yours!" And Lily took her new favorite by the arm and led him into the hotel restaurant, quite oblivious to the fact that she was dressed for a boudoir. Her grease-paint was a professional badge, justifying anything her part might call for. She took her place at the head of the table, and put Danny at her right hand, introducing him with a little speech: "This is a boy from my hometown, and don't any of you high-hat him, and don't try to question him, because I've told him not to talk."

The male star sat at Lily's other hand. He was introduced as Mr. Wallace, and asked: "Are you planning to enter the profession, Mr. Dane?" He meant it for sarcasm, and Lily shot him a fighting look, but this went clean over the head of the blue-eyed boy, who answered, cheerfully: "Oh, I'd love to, Mr. Wallace. It's been the dream of my whole life." To which the great man responded: "Ah, indeed?" and retreated into melancholy silence.

The rest of the company paid no further attention to the newcomer. Between ordering and eating their food they talked about the picture they were making and others they expected to make.

After the meal Lily took her friend to the car, and sat beside him, showing him the road, and entertaining him with the story of her career. "I'm the hometown girl that made good," she said; and went on to laugh at his admiration—while revealing her pride. She had done it by herself. "Listen, kid! This is one stinker of a town; they will put anything onto you, and unless you've got friends, or a strong nerve, they'll take everything you've got. You stick by me and I'll teach you the ropes."

The ride into Los Angeles and out to Hollywood took a couple of hours. Part of it was through traffic and required a lot of directing; but betweentimes the education of Danny went on. "You and me can have fun," said Lily, "if you'll just keep your head. One thing you have to get straight—don't you go and fall in love with me. I've had three chauffeurs make fools of themselves that way, and I had to fire them."

"I'm not going to fall in love, Lily. What I want is a career."

"I'll pay you sixty a month."

"Oh, that's too much, Lily!"

"Don't ever let those words pass your lips in Hollywood, kid. They're contrary to the code. They're treason to the profession! You gotta learn to say: 'I'm worth twice that.'"

So went the re-education of Danny Dane. The simple small-town boy would learn that the things he had admired were not what he had thought them, and he would have to get his pleasure out of despising them instead. But that would take time; for the moment he was getting his pleasure out of admiring Lily Lowe, née Gugglethwaite; and also the sights of this marvelous city, its Chinese and Mexican quarters through which they had to pass, and its maze of traffic and complicated signals and painted directions on the paving of the streets.

Presently the girl said: "We are in Hollywood. I have to tell you, because it's exactly the same as any other city."

"Oh, but the studios, Lily!"

"I'll show you one." Presently she did—a long concrete wall, with a two-story office building of stucco continuing the wall, and here and there a gate. "I know what you're thinking—the marvelous things that you'll find inside there. Well, tomorrow you can drive me in and see for yourself."

Lily's residence was modest for a star, but it appeared most sumptuous to the boy from the old hometown. In front was a Japanese gardener, sweeping a lawn with a jet from a hose. In back was a high-walled garden, with strange kinds of flowering shrubs, frequented by mockingbirds and hummingbirds; also a pond full of goldfish, and half a dozen citrus trees. Danny delivered his charge under the porte cochere, and put the car into the garage. Over the garage was a room for him, with a bath he shared only with the Chinese cook, Ling.

The rest of Lily's establishment consisted of a maid, and an elderly silent widow known as "Aunt Jenny." She was a sort of shadow relative, made necessary by the "morals clause" in the contracts of screen stars. When Lily attended any sort of public function, this "aunt" of hers was always taken along; when Lily wanted to commit any real impropriety, Aunt Jenny discreetly got out of sight and sound.

HOWARD ANSELM CAME that evening, to read Lily a passage from his revised scenario. Anselm had woven a great historical drama around a king's mistress; but the "League of Decency" was making it impossible for New York sophisticates to express themselves on the screen, and now the frightened producers insisted that King's mistresses were "out." Anselm was having to change her into a "morganatic wife," and worse, he was having to develop a tender heart in her, so that when she discovered that the welfare of the kingdom required it, she would retire to a nunnery. Her creator was suffering agonies over this humiliation, and making himself a sore trial to all those who had to do with him.

He was a tall, loose-jointed, middle-aged man, dressed with the slouchiness of the English type; that is to say, it took expensive tailoring art to achieve it. He was extremely hard to please, and all the servants feared him. He was cruel in his judgments and blunt in stating them—this in the cause of art. His witticisms were the subject of dinner-table conversations of all the screen folk. Just now his word concerning taste was law, because he was the one who could please the fastidious metropolitan critics and at the same time make money. The ex-suspender merchants and pants-pressers who ran the industry paid him a hundred dollars a minute to insult them—so Lily Lowe declared to her chauffeur.

The star herself hung upon his every gesture, for he was going to make her fame and fortune. He was going to teach her to play a new type of vamp, a pouting and kittenish one, instead of the splendid regal creatures who had sought to glorify the private life of kings.

This she explained to Danny while he was driving her to the great man's home next evening. "It's a funny kind of a life I live just now," she told him. "I'm afraid you'll be shocked if I tell you about it. But I have to tell somebody, and I can't trust people here. Will you keep my secrets—honest to goodness?"

"Sure, I don't know anybody to talk to."

"Well, here's what I'm going to do in a few minutes—take off everything except what nature put on me, and lie on a couch with pale blue silk cushions; there I'll stay while he reads me queer poetry for a couple of hours. What do you make of that?"

"Gosh!" Danny had never had to make something of anything like that in his life, and he had to think in a hurry. He didn't want to hurt Lily's feelings, and tried to find some easy way of taking it. "I hope he has the room good and warm," he ventured.

The girl began to laugh. "You funny kid! No, I haven't caught cold yet."

Danny tried to frame a delicate question. "If he's reading, he can't look at you, so why does he want you that way?"

"He says I stimulate his mood. He sprinkles perfume on me to help; some new kind he gets each day. Can you beat that?"

No, Danny couldn't. Yet he could not help judging this matter according to the standards of Missouri. Finally he asked, "Tell me, Lily—is he a good man?"

"Well, it depends on what you mean. He's a great man; and he says you can't judge great men by ordinary standards. He's a king in his own realm, so he says, and the rest seem to accept him. I'm thought to be the luckiest girl in Hollywood just now."

"What I mean is, Lily"—the other was still hesitant—"don't let him take advantage of you."

"Don't you worry about that," laughed the girl. "I'm going to get a contract to play the lead in his picture, and believe me, that contract will be read by a lawyer."

So saying, the former Miss Sally Gugglethwaite went into the hillside palace of the great writer; and her chauffeur sat in the car, or paced up and down beside it, controlling his thoughts as best he could until an hour or so after midnight, when she idly emerged under the escort of a butler in a black suit. Awed by this formality, she did not climb in beside her chauffeur, but sank back in the rear seat with a dignity which became the future morganatic wife of a king. Danny started the car; and when they were out of sight in the darkness he heard her voice: "Stop a minute. Let me get in by you." He stopped; and when they were underway again she said: "I'm lonesome, and I'm scared. Danny, can you imagine?"

"What?"

"He wants me to marry him!"

Danny caught his breath. "Well, but, Lily—that'll make it all right, won't it?"

"You think so? Of course, from the professional point of view, it's marvelous. I'll be number one ace in the studio. I can pick my own roles—or, rather, he will pick them for me. But, Danny—it'll be awful!"

"How do you mean?"

"Can I bear to be tied to a man like that? It'll be so queer—all those things that he does! And the way he lives! I'll have to be so God-awful elegant."

"Doesn't he love you as you are?"

"Not a bit of it; he loves me because he wants to make me what he is. All men are like that."

———

LILY LOWE WAS JUSTIFIED in her prediction that this marriage would give a boost to her career. In between interviews with the press she was in conference with her lawyers who were negotiating her contract for the new picture, at a price so enormous nobody would believe it when they heard it—which of course they did at once.

She went to live in the hillside mansion of her new husband. Her old home was rented, and the rent had a couple of weeks to run, so Danny stayed where he was, as did the other servants, except Lily's maid. Aunt Jenny, of course, did not have to be told the services of a chaperone would no longer be needed, and she began seeking a new position.

In the meantime, Danny helped to pack the star's belongings and carry them to her new home in the car; and answered the telephone, stating, according to instructions, that he was Miss Lowe's secretary, and that all messages, no matter how confidential, were to be delivered to him. Lily's was supposed to be a "nonlist" number, but everybody in Hollywood appeared to have it, and everybody had read about her new contract, and either wanted to interview her for a chain of newspapers in Sweden, or to invite her to dinner, or to sell her stocks and bonds, or a new kind of electric refrigerator, or an airplane, or a tract of land in British Columbia, or a scenario based on the love life of Hindu adepts.

Aunt Jenny had the duty of answering the doorbell, by way of paying for her keep; she took to sitting on the front porch, to repel the enemy before they got to the steps. One afternoon she came to Danny with some signs of agitation, and said: "Mr. Dane, there's a woman out there that I can't get rid of. Perhaps you better talk to her."

Danny was an experienced man of the world by now. He knew all the queer kinds of people, and the subterfuges they employed, and the devices by which one persuaded them to be satisfied with nothing. He went out to the front porch, drawn up to his full height, and trying to look and act twice his years; he closed the door behind him, and then said to the persistent lady: "Good day, madame. I am Miss Lowe's secretary. What can I do for you?"

"You can't do anything for me," was the prompt answer. "I have to see Miss Lowe."

She was a woman of forty or so, brunette, with the memory of beauty upon her; but now she was thin and haggard, with dark shadows under her eyes. She was not shabby, but on the other hand not fashionably dressed. She was evidently laboring under strain, and there was a suggestion of wildness about her.

"Do you know Miss Lowe?" asked the secretary.

"I have never seen her; but I have something urgent to see her about—something of importance to her."

Said Danny, who had watched and listened to the secretaries of magnates and presidents and other master of affairs on the screen: "Madame, I am sorry, but I have my orders from Miss Lowe. You will have to tell me your business before I can even consider making an appointment."

"But Miss Lowe herself would not wish anyone else to know what I have to tell her."

"Madame, I have to explain I am not merely Miss Lowe's confidential secretary, I am her cousin and her best friend. She has no secrets from me, and I assure you whatever you say will not be divulged."

The woman stared, as if trying to peer into the boy's soul. She began twisting her handbag, and she looked around to see if there was anybody in hearing distance; then, glaring at him in sudden defiance, she said: "All right, if you must have it. Call Miss Lowe at the studio and tell her that Mrs. Howard Anselm wishes to see her."

A queer look came into Danny's face. "But Miss Lowe is Mrs. Howard Anselm."

"Well, I got ahead of her. I have been Mrs. Howard Anselm for more than twenty years."

So Danny had a problem such as he had never seen handled by any private secretary of a magnate or president or other master of affairs. He pondered it for a bit, and then said: "All right, madame. If you will come inside, I will try to get word to Miss Lowe."

He escorted the woman to the drawing room, then went upstairs and shut himself in. He called the studio and, being told that Lily was in conference, stated it was urgent, and he must speak to her.

When he heard her voice, he said: "Lily, there's something very serious at the house. I wouldn't call you like this if I could help it."

"What is it, Danny?"

"You wouldn't want me to say it over the phone. You had better drop whatever you are doing, and come to the house."

"Well, for God's sake, Danny..." Lily's voice died away; she was frightened, of course. "All right, I'll come."

Danny hung up. In the midst of his concern, something was dancing in him. The Golden Scenario! He was in the midst of it now; never anything to beat it!

Lily had told him that she kept a gun in her desk drawer; he thought it the better part of wisdom to find and slip it into his coat pocket. He went down to the drawing room, where the first Mrs. Howard Anselm sat nervously tapping her foot on the Kandahar rug made in Michigan. "I have told Miss Lowe," he said. "She will come at once."

"Thank you," said the woman; and no more.

When Lily returned to her former abode half an hour later, Danny met her in the hall, and escorted the ladies to Lily's boudoir. "Now, Cousin Lily," he said, "this lady will tell you her story."

The lady did it in one sentence. "Nearly twenty-one years ago, Howard Anselm and I were married in Greenwich, Connecticut."

"Oh, my God!" said Lily.

"We lived as husband and wife for more than ten years. All his friends in New York knew me as his wife."

"Can you prove that?"

"I have the marriage certificate with me."

"Let me see it," said Lily.

The woman took a paper from her handbag. "I want this back!" she admonished.

"Don't be silly," was the other's reply. "If the thing is genuine, you can easily get another copy."

"It's genuine, all right," said the first Mrs. Anselm. "What would I come way out here for?"

Lily took the paper and studied it, then handed it back.

"You've never been divorced?"

"Never."

"Well," said the actress, "that's a fine mess. Apparently I'm a bigamist."

"I'm not thinking of that."

"What do you want? Money?"

"No. I wanted to tell you about it. We're both of us victims of the same scoundrel. We have to decide what to do."

"Tell me about yourself," said Lily.

"My name is Agnes Hyatt. I was a clerk in a bank and he was a newspaper reporter when we met. I was young, and I gave him my youth, my beauty. I made a home for him, I entertained his friends, and made others for him. I suffered and starved while he learned to be a writer. I denied myself children, I ruined my health; I did everything that a woman could do for a man. Then, when he made a success, when he was rich and famous—then he had to have other women; his development as a writer required it. And I was a fool—I loved him, and I stood everything. But finally he couldn't stand me anymore, and he left. I refused his money; I went to work again, I took care of myself. I have never bothered him. But then, I read in the paper that he had married a young girl; the same story all over again. I said, It's her right to know. He wrecked my youth— he shan't wreck hers."

The woman had been speaking with mounting excitement, and now sobs were shaking her. This, of course, is contagious; or possibly it may have occurred to the second Mrs. Anselm that some demonstration was called for. After all, she was an emotional actress, and had to practice many roles. She put her hands to her face and covered it, and began to weep softly. Later on she sank down upon the sofa, and buried her head entirely, and shook with weeping. Danny stood, tears of sympathy running down his cheeks—but also not forgetting that this was the Golden Scenario, and he was in it!

Presently the downpour ceased and the floods dried. Said Lily: "What are we going to do?"

"One or the other of us has got to punish him," said Agnes. "Will you?"

Lily thought it over. "I don't see how I can," she said, finally. "I've just signed a contract to make a picture."

"Are you willing for me to see him?"

"Of course. Why not?"

"Remember, this is serious."

There was a silence. Danny watched one face, then the other. The ending of the Golden Scenario was being decided. Would Lily plead for her lover? Lily did not.

"Where is he?" asked Agnes, suddenly.

Lily of course didn't have to answer that question. But she said: "He's at home, working on some changes in the story."

The other woman got up. "All right," she said, with decision. "That's all. Thanks for being polite." And out she went.

After Danny had escorted the first Mrs. Anselm to the front door, the second Mrs. Anselm called him upstairs again, and shut the door. "Danny," she said, "you know this is a dead-serious matter. That woman has guts."

"I know it," agreed Danny.

"I'll need a lawyer—and no piker either. That contract of mine has been in the papers; and you may be sure the police have read it, and the district attorney's office. If Howard Anselm should get hurt, they'll do anything—absolutely anything—to put it onto me. They'll hit me for a hundred grand—not a dollar less."

They went downstairs, and Lily called in Aunt Jenny and Ling.

"Now," she said, "this is what. I've got a headache. Those people are trying to work me to death at the studio. What's the use of a lot of money if you make yourself ill? I came home. I'm going to enjoy life. Ling, you know how to play croquet?"

"Cloquet?" echoed Ling. "You cook him?"

"I'll show you," said Lily. "We'll have fun. Danny, I saw an old set in the garage. We'll put it up."

So out into the beautiful walled garden went the screen star, with her boy cousin, and her elderly chaperone, and her fat Chinese cook, with his grin wider than ever. Danny got the box with the croquet set in it, and they put up the wickets.

Such was the scene when a busy lawyer arrived from downtown, having canceled his appointments. To his still greater surprise, he was told that he looked as if he too had been overworking, and needed to play croquet; Aunt Jenny was tired, so would he take her place?

Of course a motion-picture lawyer learns all about the whims of leading ladies, and may be thankful if one orders him to do nothing more unpleasant than play a game in a beautiful garden on a sunshiny afternoon. When he knows that he has just drawn up an ironclad contract for her, and witnessed the signatures, he permits her to enjoy his company. He proved a good player, and was in the midst of explaining the angles of a croquet shot when the butler at the Anselm home telephoned the information that he had just found Mrs. Anselm's husband lying on the floor of his study with a bullet through his heart.

Of course the lawyer, being no "piker," changed his mind about this croquet game. He took charge of the situation, and while Lily wept softly on her couch, he questioned the butler. The man had not admitted anybody to the home, nor seen anybody enter or leave; so evidently it was a case of suicide. The lawyer told the butler not to notify the police, and not to disturb anything in the house. Then he phoned to his office for a couple of his associates; then to the studio for a couple of their lawyers. He told Aunt Jenny to lock all the doors, and let nobody in except those lawyers.

Then he shut himself in the room with Danny and Lily, and asked them for the story. He whistled when he heard about the other woman; that changed the face of the thing. It would be better not to say anything about her; she had apparently made a getaway, and the police need never know about her.

The real story was obvious, this competent lawyer told his client. Howard Anselm was impotent; a literary man, living an ascetic life, he found that he could not be a husband, and overcome by humiliation, and a sense of the wrong he had done his young wife, he had taken himself out of her way. That was a good, clean story; nothing in it to violate the "morals clause," or injure Lily's "box office." The studio people would agree to that. Lily must deny herself to all callers, and be overcome with grief. The only problem was, could they trust Aunt Jenny not to mention the visit of Agnes? Lily thought she could be "fixed," and the lawyer went downstairs to perform the operation.

The other lawyers arrived, and checked and approved the story. Then they went over to Anselm's house, and from there notified the police. Soon after that the deluge broke; the story of the suicide of the screen star's husband went by telegraph and cable to every corner of the world except the two poles, and a few spots in the forests of the Amazon and of New Guinea.

Everything was "oke," as they say in Hollywood, except for one dreadful blunder which Danny made. He thought it would do no harm for him to slip out a side door and get the newspaper.

But just as he stopped to pick it up, hands fell on each of his shoulders, and he glanced up and saw two stern-looking men. "Come on, kid," said one. "We want you." And before he could get his wits together they were running him out to the street, where a car stood at the curb.

He had no time even to make up his mind whether he ought to yell or not; they shoved him into the car, and one sprang in beside him, and put a firm restraining arm around his neck. "Keep still, kid; we're the police. We know that somebody killed Howard Anselm, and we know that you know who it was. Make up your mind, you're going to come clean, or be torn all to bits. Now, last call! Will you tell?"

"I...I don't..." whispered Danny. And suddenly the man threw himself on Danny; he caught him by the throat, and the two of them went down together. The boy was suffocating; he tried to scream; he struggled, he kicked out madly, he made frantic efforts to lift the mountain load which seemed to be crushing the breath out of him. Then he heard a sound, a loud sound, as of someone pounding on a wooden wall. He heard a voice, stern and commanding. "What's the matter with you there? Shut up that racket."

Somehow the weight seemed to be lifting; the grasp of the detectives weakened, the agony grew less, and fear gave place to bewilderment. For that was the voice of old Mr. Givers, the Spanish War veteran, shouting. "Shut up, boy, you're waking the whole house!"

Danny found that he could get the bedclothes untwisted from his face, and he raised up, and called through the partition, "Yes, all right." The whole nightmare was gone, all but the trembling and the bath of perspiration. He was in his bed in the attic of Aunt Anna's boardinghouse. As for Hollywood, and all that strange story—could it be that he had dreamed all that? Danny wanted to go back and dream that dream some more. But then another thought: the Golden Scenario! Yes, he had it: the BID IDEA! He must hang onto it; write it down before he forgot it!

He looked out. Dawn was just breaking behind the great bulk of the cheese factory. He got up, trembling still with excitement, and found a pencil and paper, and propped himself up with his pillow, and began to trace back that fast-fading dream. "How strange! I made all that up about little Sally Gugglethwaite, that I used to think I was in love with! And all that bad stuff about Hollywood—where did I get that? Oh yes, a magazine article that Professor Henniger had told us about; it made us all mad, and Miss Betts said the man that wrote it was a sorehead!"

When Danny crept downstairs to make the kitchen fire that morning, he had the Golden Scenario clear in his mind. He was so wrapped up in it that he was nearly run over by an automobile on the way to school, so completely was he living the story of Lily Lowe and Agnes Hyatt. He was mysterious with the boarders, giving them no hint that they were to figure in the work. He kept the secret until close to the end of his task; then spasms of doubt began to afflict him, and first he decided he ought to avail himself of the literary skill of Professor Henniger; after all, this was the great chance of Danny's life, and it would be too bad to lose it through the crudities of his writing.

He invited the professor to read his manuscript; and when he found that the professor didn't object to being in the story, Danny decided that he ought to have the advantage of Miss Pansy Betts' intimate knowledge of the mysteries of the feminine heart. Then he made use of Mr. Wink's longstanding acquaintance with the more reckless and outspoken portions of the sex.

So on until, before he got through, Danny had all the boarders reading and criticizing the merits of his scenario. It was not that any of these conscientious persons would deliberately steal any of Danny's original ideas; but they were all trying to think up ideas of their own, and Danny's were so much better, that naturally they dominated the minds of the boarders, and it wasn't long before they were each secretly convinced that they too had been contemplating a scenario about people in a boardinghouse. Thus six or eight versions of the Golden Scenario were born.

BUT LET US FOLLOW the main thread, which is the script entitled *Ho for Hollywood*, by Danny Dane, submitted to the National Screen Writers Agency of Hollywood. It was opened by Operator 17, who first made sure there was a name and address on the manuscript, and then attached to it a slip bearing the date of receipt, and her own number, and a file number of the script. She then laid it in a

CREATING POPULAR CULTURE   133

wire tray, which presently was taken by Operator 9, a typist, who wrote a personal letter to Danny Dane, 158 South Muskingam Street, Johannesburg, Missouri, informing him that his scenario had been received, and would be duly considered for the prize, and he would hear from the agency promptly. Operator 9 wrote 48 such letters every day of her young life. This was known as No. 1 Letter, and Operator 9 marked the slip to indicate that this letter had been sent, and then put the manuscript into another wire basket, to be passed on to Operator 26.

This operator was known as the "reader," and she read one hundred manuscripts per day, which meant that to each one she gave an average of five minutes. For the great majority a hurried glance, perhaps a half a minute, sufficed; they were pitiful products of minds with no talent, competence, or originality of any sort. In such cases Operator 26 put her number on the slip, followed by the letter "N," which was an abbreviation for "N.G." Such manuscripts were stacked according to date, and waited one week before they were taken out in order and laid upon the desk of another typist, who wrote what was known as the No. 2 Letter, also a personal communication informing the author that the National Screen Writers Agency had considered the manuscript submitted; that it had been found to contain very unusual qualities, and to hold out promise for its author; but that unfortunately from the technical point of view it was not in such shape that it could be submitted to the studios. The agency was fortunate in having the services of trained writers, who would be glad to furnish their help in preparing the manuscript, after which it would be duly submitted.

The letter added that of course the agency could not guarantee that any studio would accept the script, but they would do their best. It closed with the hope that the writer would decide promptly, as this was the time of year when the manuscript market was active. The cost of the service was the merely nominal sum of ten dollars.

This letter also figured to take ten minutes to write. Altogether the cost of handling these "N" manuscripts was found to be 18.54

cents per script, and the overhead of the agency was figured at 11.63 per script. It was found that No. 2 Letter brought replies from 22.71 percent of the cases, from which it appears that No. 2 Letter brought a net profit of a trifle over $1.97 per script. When you learn that the National Screen Writers Agency handled 34,549 "N" manuscripts in the year 1934, you can understand why it could spend large sums for advertising in national publications.

We continue with *Ho for Hollywood*, by Danny Dane, which was last found in the hands of Operator 26. She marked it "G. 7, 14, 28"—which meant she had noted something good on those three pages. Another operator received it, and wrote the No. 4 Letter, which was one of more cordial praise, promising far more careful service, for which a charge of twenty-five dollars was made. Danny read this letter with rapture, collected all his savings, and persuaded his devoted and hardworking aunt to lend him fourteen dollars. Having sent the money, he received in reply the No. 9 Letter—he had got up into the higher brackets now—informing him his script was being revised; and after two weeks, he received the No. 10 Letter, enclosing the new version for his inspection.

This version consisted of Danny's story written in the technical language of the studios: "distance shots," "closeups," "dissolves," "we fade here to such-and-such," "we cut to so-and-so," "we pan to something else." This rewriting had been done by an operator who was paid fifty cents an hour for the ability to use these various phrases, whether rightly or wrongly no one knew or cared. This typing job took a trifle over four hours, and allowing for overhead, the agency's profit on the "G" letters was close to a hundred thousand dollars per year.

Danny was furthermore informed that his script had been submitted to a studio; and this was strictly true. The post-office authorities came frequently to investigate the affairs of the National Screen Writers Agency; they scrutinized all its advertising and its form letters, but were never able to point out where it had failed to do anything promised. Danny's revised script, in an envelope with forty-two others, was sent by registered mail to the studio of Magnificent Pictures Inc.; a studio which, having had many suits for plagiarism, made an invariable rule to return all unsolicited scripts without opening the envelopes. This concern, of course, had no way to keep National Agency from sending it mail; the agency duly sent return postage, and of course kept all registry receipts, and thus could prove what it had done.

The "G" scripts came next to the office of Miss Gladys Watcome, who was so important in the establishment that she was known by name rather than by number. Miss Watcome had three readers who really knew their jobs, and looked over everything which had been specially marked. For there was always a chance, among the mass of mediocrity, that a real find might occur.

The junior agency partner was Jake Zinsenstein, who knew studios and stars and stories. Also his wife was an avid reader, and liked the "picture game"; she ran, under her maiden name, a sort of secondary agency, selling the really good ideas that came in. She had no less than seven writers under contract; she furnished ideas, and they wrote, and went 50-50 with her on their contracts. This money Maida Zinsenstein faithfully turned in to the agency, and got back her share as dividends on her stock. "People just have to be able to trust each other," said Maida.

A carbon copy of *Ho for Hollywood*, by Danny Dane, came over in due course to the Zinsenstein home, and Maida discussed its ideas with Eddie Benedict, ex-jockey turned screenwriter. They agreed the story of Lily Lowe would not do—it was, as Eddie said, "too true to be good." But the idea of a boardinghouse full of film fans, and a kid writing a scenario and coming to Hollywood—that wasn't bad. Eddie changed the locale to New York City, and made all the boarders into New York types. He also decided Danny would have more sex appeal if he was a girl.

Eddie wrote a sketch of this story, and Maida sent it to Larry Prichett, a director for Excelsior, suggesting that it might make a part for Bessie Bennett. But Larry already had a story for Bessie, and passed on the idea to Dave Orcutt, head of the studio, who was looking for a part for a Hawaiian dancer whom he had met on his last trip, and to whom he was under certain obligations. Dave sent for Eddie, and asked if he didn't think it might be possible to place his story in a company boardinghouse on a sugar plantation in Hawaii, to which Eddie said, Sure, why not? He didn't know anything about Hawaii, but Dave said he could borrow a print of *The Bird of Paradise* and run it for Eddie; and besides, he had a guidebook, and Hula—that was the dancer—could tell him the rest.

So Eddie spent four days getting the local color of Hawaii, and wrote the script, and Maida sold it to Dave for $12,000, and Dave paid one of his studio men another $9,000 to rewrite it. It was a "quickie," and was shot in two weeks and a half, its total cost on the books of Excelsior being $115,000. You can see it in the third-run houses now, if you yourself are a "quickie"; it is called *Bloodbeat*, and is one of those pictures which do not try to get the imprimatur of the Catholic film censors. The picture played a day and a night at the Rialto Theater, and Danny's Aunt Anna didn't want him to go; but it happened to be Friday night, and he begged so hard— after all, he was a screenwriter now, they had made an investment in the industry, and he must know what was going on.

So Danny saw the Hollywood version of his Golden Scenario. He found it thrilling; and one detail gave him a particular thrill. For when the Hawaiian dancer has stabbed the banker's son who has betrayed her love, and wants to hide her trail, she gets the servants in her household out into the garden and has them teach her to play croquet. Danny went home in a state of excitement, and told the boarders about it. "Somebody stole that idea from my script!"

They discussed the possibility all through breakfast, and that evening Danny wrote a letter to the National Screen Writers Agency, and a week or two later received a copy of No. 25 Letter, typed by Operator 14. The agency assured Mr. Dane that they took every precaution to protect the rights of their authors. They submitted scripts only to the most reliable producers. Of course it might happen that two persons would sometimes think of the same idea; such cases had been proved in court proceedings. The agency suggested that Mr. Dane might care to protect his scenario by copywriting it, and if he so desired the agency would be pleased to attend to the matter for him for a fee of five dollars.

Danny didn't have the money, and since old Mrs. Hooper was still paralyzed he had no way to earn it. He read the letter to the boarders, and discussed it. Danny said, after all, he supposed it might be possible for someone else to think of a game of croquet; and Miss Pansy Betts was much relieved to hear this—because she had used that idea in her scenario, and had just received a copy of the "N" Letter, and had sent a post-office order for ten dollars, so that her script might have a chance to be adjudged the Golden Scenario. Miss Betts suffered qualms of conscience for many weeks, lest her script win and Danny think she had broken faith with him.

But the fears proved groundless, for Miss Betts never heard any more about her Golden Scenario, and Danny never heard any more about his, and the two of them are the best of friends, and in fact are now cooperating on a new script having to do with a grand opera singer in St. Petersburg before the revolution. Danny is now having dreams about this singer, and when he and Miss Betts refer to the Golden Scenario, it is this one they have in mind.

from "Comes the Moment to Decide"
Book Two of A World to Win,
World's End Series, 1946

> I wish I were terribly rich, I wish I had an inexhaustible quantity
> of paper: for I would supply a whole set of the Lanny Budd
> novels to every boy and girl graduating from high school. I think
> they would then have a better chance of entering the adult
> world with an understanding grasp of what life holds for them.
> —Irving Stone, An Upton Sinclair Anthology, 1947

IN 1938, THE SINCLAIRS heard the radio report of Hitler's invasion
of Czechoslovakia. Mary Craig said, "Well, our world is at an end.
I don't see how anyone can fail to realize that."[1] Six weeks later,
Sinclair had a vision of the entire World's End series: "Walking in
my garden one night, something happened; a spring was touched,
a button pressed...There was no resisting it, and I didn't try."[2]
The series that resulted would be Sinclair's greatest contribution to
popular culture. Titled "World's End," it is often referred to by its
readers as the Lanny Budd series.[3]

Fascinated with the ways in which educated and privileged people
respond to social injustice, Sinclair confided that "Lanny Budd was
a dream boy. He was a combination of a number of well-to-do
young idealists whom I had known."[4] Sinclair's idea was that "the
hero would learn, just as [Sinclair] hoped his readers would, that
fascism was a menace to world peace and could not be ignored but
must be destroyed."[5]

Critic Sally Parry calls Lanny Budd "the Allies' secret weapon
against the Third Reich."[6] The first novel, World's End, begins in
1911; the last, O Shepherd Speak!, is set at the close of World War II.
Its hero is the sensitive and idealistic son of Robert Budd, an
American arms manufacturer. Relationships shaped by access to
wealth and his expertise in fine art enable Lanny to move freely

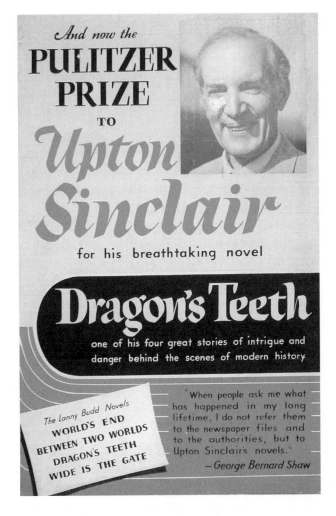

And now the
PULITZER PRIZE
TO
Upton Sinclair

for his breathtaking novel

Dragon's Teeth

one of his four great stories of intrigue and danger behind the scenes of modern history

The Lanny Budd Novels
WORLD'S END
BETWEEN TWO WORLDS
DRAGON'S TEETH
WIDE IS THE GATE

"When people ask me what has happened in my long lifetime, I do not refer them to the newspaper files and to the authorities, but to Upton Sinclair's novels."
—George Bernard Shaw

Dragon's Teeth is the third novel of the Worlds End series. Theodore Dreiser wrote Sinclair: "Talk about novelized history, economics, sociology, greed, and why not! Here they strut the stage as characters."

into Germany before and after Hitler's rise to power. Theodore Dreiser, after reading the first volume, wrote, "Talk about novelized history, economics, sociology, greed and what not! Here they strut the stage as characters."[7] The first eight novels sold over one million copies in the United States alone and were translated into twenty languages. Historian Perry Miller wrote, "Sighing like Lanny over the muddle of the world, I eagerly await my next installment."[8]

The World's End series has had a complex history as a Hollywood project. Helen Taubkin, secretary to actor Tyrone Power in the 1940s, writes: "I read and enjoyed the entire Lanny Budd series. I even tried to persuade Tyrone Power to have the studio buy the series as a starring vehicle for him."[9] The studio's antipathy toward Sinclair after his campaign for governor may have buried this project. Although the series was optioned for television in 1962, screenwriter Malvin Wald believes that when Sinclair wrote to *Newsweek* condemning Henry Ford's business dealings with the Nazis, the Ford Motor Company's sponsorship was lost."[10]

Upton Sinclair received the Pulitzer Prize for *Dragon's Teeth*, the third novel in the series, in 1942. Pulitzer juror John Chamberlain wrote, "Almost alone among our novelists, he has realized that contemporary history, as it comes through to us every day in the headlines, has become so overpowering that many individuals can have no significant emotional life apart from it." Like the writer Julius Epstein, who created in *Casablanca* a challenge to isolationism, Sinclair's World's End series profoundly affected the American public's willingness to join the war: it was what Dieter Herms describes as "antifascist propaganda entertainingly packaged in the wrappers of popular literature."[11]

In the excerpt included here from *A World to Win*, the seventh book in the series, Lanny Budd is working as an agent for Roosevelt; he has had intimate visits with Hitler and often uses the Nazi interest in psychics to get information.[12] He comes to California to get information about both the Hollywood community and William Randolph Hearst.

Notes

1. Upton Sinclair, cable to *Pravda* (Upton Sinclair Archives, Lilly Library at Indiana University, Bloomington Indiana), October 14, 1938

2. Upton Sinclair, "World's End Impending," published in 1940, reprinted in *O Shepherd, Speak!* (New York: Viking, 1949)

3. Germaine Warkentin, professor of English at the University of Toronto, writes: "The Lanny Budd books were my introduction to modern history. I simply

devoured them, over the summers of 1947 and 1948." (personal correspondence, Warkentin to Coodley, January 17, 1997)

4. Ron Gottesman, Interview with Upton Sinclair, Columbia Oral History Project, 1962–1963

5. Sally Parry, "Learning to Fight the Nazis: The Education of Upton Sinclair's Lanny Budd" in *Visions of War: World War II in Popular Culture and Literature*, ed. M. Paul Holsinger and Mary Anne Scholfield (Bowling Green, Ohio: Popular Press, 1992), 257

6. Sally Parry, "Upton Sinclair's Lanny Budd: The Allies' Secret Weapon against the Third Reich" in *Germany and German Thought in American Literature and Cultural Criticism*, ed. Peter Freese (Essen: Verlag Die Blaue Eule, 1990). Sally Parry believes Lanny was similar to Putzi Hanfstaengel, a Harvard graduate who was kept in Hitler's entourage to entertain but was secretly advising the United States. Sinclair commented in his autobiography that: "I actually knew a Presidential agent and he helped with Lanny Budd. This was Cornelius Vanderbilt Jr.—we met him early in California when he was trying to start a liberal newspaper in a reactionary community"

7. Quoted in Mike Riherd, "Upton Sinclair: Creating 'World's End,'" (Ph.D. dissertation, University of Southern California, 1978), 7

8. Perry Miller, "Lanny Budd Rides Again," *New York Times*, August 20, 1948, review of *One Clear Call.* Later Miller wrote Sinclair that "I was brought up by a Socialist father and I believe that almost the first writer beyond the kindergarten level to whom I was introduced was Upton Sinclair." (December 10, 1952, cited in Leon Harris, *Upton Sinclair: American Rebel* (New York: Thomas Crowell, 1975), 409

9. Personal correspondence, Helen Taubkin to Coodley, January 23, 1996

10. Lauren Coodley, Interview with Malvin Wald, July 23, 1996

11. Dieter Herms, "An American Socialist: Upton Sinclair" in *The Upton Beall Sinclair Centenary Journal* 1:1, September 1978, 52. Herms, born in 1937, was a child during the Nazi era.

12. See Upton Sinclair, *Mental Radio* (Charlottesville, Va.: Hampton Roads, 1930), 201. Mary Craig Sinclair was fascinated by psychic phenomena and persuaded Sinclair to document their personal experiments in extrasensory perception. Albert Einstein wrote the preface to the book.

LANNY CROSSED THE Colorado River by a long bridge, and was in the California desert, near the Death Valley region. It was having a hot spell now, and he had been advised to pass through at night. He couldn't see the landscape, but judged that it must be flat and level, for the road went straight, like a great steel tape stretched taut. The car lights shone on it, far ahead, and exercised a hypnotic effect—but it was better not to nod, bowling along at a mile a minute. A hot, almost suffocating wind blew upon him and seemed to be drying the blood in his veins; doubtless he was perspiring, but there was no trace upon him. A strange thing to drive into the little town of Baker, and discover broad paved streets, and filling stations and other places ablaze with light, and realize that human beings lived in this heat, not merely by night but by day! Lanny, a considerate person, didn't want to discourage them, and forbore to ask how they stood it.

He drove until he was in the orange country. He stopped at a town called Riverside—but its river was dry; he put up at a hotel called the Mission Inn—but there was no mission, only a museum full of California curiosities. He had a good sleep, and then drove through miles and miles of orange and lemon groves, laden with golden and yellow fruit. The towns had picturesque names: Pomona, which was Greek, Azusa, which was Indian, Monrovia and Pasadena, which had come out of some realtor's dream.

So he came to Hollywood, his goal for the moment, and the dream of all movie fans from China to Peru. The town had been taken into the sprawling city of Los Angeles, most of the studios had moved into the near-by valleys, and the actors had their homes everywhere but in Hollywood; so it was no longer a geographical location but merely a trademark. The landscape and climate reminded Lanny of the Côte d'Azur; but there he had never seen "supermarkets" with all the fruits and vegetables of the world spread out, nor "drive-in eateries" nor "hotdog stands" and "orange juiceries" built in the shape of Indian tepees or Eskimo igloos or sitting white cats or other Mother Goose or Walt Disney creations. It was, he discovered, like all California towns, built haphazard, a jumble of anybody's whims, with half its spaces empty because people were holding them, waiting for values to rise.

WHILE DRIVING LANNY had been thinking of who in this region might serve his underground purpose. Sooner or later "everybody" came here, and many of them stayed. In the course of his life he had met journalists, writers, musicians, actors—hundreds of them in his mother's home, other hundreds while he and Irma had been playing about in café society in New York, and yet others while Irma had been playing the salonnière in Paris. Many he had forgotten, and many, no doubt, had forgotten him; but his memory lighted upon a couple, the De Lyle Armbrusters, who had "scads" of money and had amused themselves all over the world; he had run into them at the Savoy in London, and again at the Adlon in Berlin, and in Algiers when they had been on a yachting trip. Irma had mentioned that they had settled in Beverly Hills, and Lanny guessed that wherever they were they would know the celebrities.

He looked them up in the fat Los Angeles telephone book and there they were. He called the number, and a grave English voice answered. In smart society the only grave voice is that of the butler, so Lanny said: "Is either Mr. or Mrs. Armbruster at home?" The reply was: "Whom shall I say, sir?"—in smart society the only persons who bother with grammar are the butler and the social secretary. Lanny answered: "Tell them, please, that Mr. Lanny Budd is calling."

In half a moment more there was Genie, short for Eugenia, bubbling over with welcome. "Lanny, how perfectly ducky! Where are you?"

"I'm at the Beverly-Wilshire."

"Oh, you darling, how nice! We'll be having cocktails—won't you run over? Any time from five to seven—and stay for dinner and we'll chew the rag."

That's the way it is when you know the "right" people, you just don't have any troubles at all, unless you drink too many cocktails, or make love to your host's wife. Lanny had time to bathe and shave, and glance at an afternoon paper to see that London still survived. His clothes, freshly pressed, were brought to his door, and his car, freshly washed and serviced, was brought to the door of the hotel. The porter told him how to get to Benedict Canyon. There he found an Italian Renaissance villa of some twenty rooms, built on the side of a mountain, so that things above and below it had to be terraced and walled to keep them from sliding down. It was just like the heights above Cannes, or the place called Californie above Nice, where the Duke and Duchess of Windsor had been staying. There was a tennis court and a swimming pool, and from the loggia you looked over the whole Los Angeles plain, the blue Pacific, and the Channel Islands beyond. At night it was a vast plain, a bowl full of lights, an unequaled spectacle.

———————

EVERYWHERE IN THE modern world are rich people trying to escape boredom, and willing to keep open house for anybody who can produce a novelty. If they are very rich they do it on a grand scale and the drive in front of their home and the road outside will be lined with a double row of motorcars. Some specialize in "headliners," and go to any trouble to secure their presence. The "headliners" may be rich, too, but they have to work for their money, whereas the rich rich can make a business of hospitality. As a reward their names are always in the society columns and everybody knows who they are. De Lyle Armbruster was fiftyish and stoutish, as bland and smiling as the headwaiter in the dining-room of a "palace hotel." His wife, blond and animated, was Lanny's age, supposedly dangerous for women; she kissed him and called him "old dear," and was as glad to see him as if he had still been Mister Irma Barnes.

All proper homes now have a private bar gleaming with chromium, or maybe platinum—who can be sure? The room will be done in jazz colors, or paintings in the surrealist style; there may be photographs signed by celebrity friends, or original copies of cartoons from the great centers of politics and culture. The guests stand about, nibble tiny sausages and other delicacies stuck on toothpicks, sip drinks with torpedo and brimstone names, and chat about the price which not more than an hour ago was paid for the picture rights of the newest best-seller, scheduled for publication next week. Or perhaps it will be the seven-year contract which the speaker has just been offered but hasn't yet decided about; or the star who has been chosen to play the role of Joan of Arc or President Wilson. So you will know that you are in Hollywood.

The first person to whom Lanny Budd was introduced was Charles Laughton, whom he had previously known as King Henry the Eighth; the second was another round-faced and beaming gentleman, Charles Coburn, whom he had seen in comedies, always as a millionaire father perplexed by the insane behavior of his children. On the screen these personages were enlarged to god-like proportions and their voices filled a great theater. To meet them now, reduced to ordinary size, to shake hands with them and discover that they were made of flesh and blood, was an experience like walking into the Mermaid Tavern and being presented to Will Shakespeare and Ben Jonson. How does one address such supernal beings? What can one say, of admiration and awe, which they have not heard from a thousand autograph-hungry fans?

Lanny could say: "I saw you in Athens, and again in the town of Stubendorf, in Upper Silesia." That was slightly better. He could say to Bette Davis: "It might interest you to know that Hitler showed me *Dark Victory* in his home at Berchtesgaden." It did interest her, and she asked what the Führer had said. That was what Lanny wanted; for almost at once he became the center of a group plying him with questions. People in Hollywood found it as extraordinary to meet someone who had been in the same room with Hitler as Lanny found it to be in the same room with Charles Laughton and Bette Davis. How did Hitler talk, and what did he eat, and what sort of table manners did he have? Was he really quite sane? And what about his love life? Above all, was he going to be able to knock out London?

AT ONE SIDE OF the ample drawing-room was a large overstuffed chair which bore a certain resemblance to a throne, and on it sat a round-faced ample lady who bore a certain resemblance to a queen in the movies. She rarely moved, but people came to her and made obeisance and paid tribute in the form of news: what they had done that day and what they were planning to do, what their friends had done—in short all the gossip of the studios they had chanced to pick up: who was now keeping company with whom, who was expecting a baby, or a divorce, or an elopement. They were all her friends, and they all called her Louella, and all she exacted in return was that they would give her an "exclusive." Woe betide them if they ever broke faith with her on this all-important point!

It was rare indeed that anybody ever "stole the show" from this queen of publicity, and she frowned as she observed the phenomenon. To the hostess she addressed the question: "Who is that fellow that is talking so much?"

The hostess was glad to explain, for it might be worth a paragraph, and the De Lyle Armbrusters might be mentioned in it. "His name is Lanny Budd. He used to be the husband of Irma Barnes, the heiress who was the glamour girl of Broadway some ten or twelve years ago."

"I read the newspapers," replied Louella coldly.

"His father is Budd-Erling Aircraft," added the other, putting first things first. "The son is a very distinguished art expert."

"Why does everybody want to hear about art all of a sudden?"

"It isn't that, Louella. It so happens he is a personal friend of Hitler, and has recently been visiting him."

"Can that really be true?"

"He knows Göring and Hess, and all the leading Nazis. He has been Göring's art adviser for many years. He was with them in Paris when the armistice was signed."

"Well, Genie, what is the matter with you? Why haven't you introduced him to me?"

"I didn't know whether you'd be interested, Louella. His pictures aren't the kind that move."

"Good God, am I never to talk anything but shop? And besides, the man looks like a movie actor. He'd make another Ronald Colman. Somebody ought to give him a screen test!"

The hostess needed to hear no more. She went over and broke into the circle, interrupting a description of the Berghof. "I want to introduce you to somebody," she said, and of course that was a command. Lanny followed her, and the others came along; they must have been troubled by the discourtesy they were showing to their publicity queen. "Louella Parsons," said Genie, "this is Lanny Budd."

There was one chair, placed so that one person could be seated in front of the throne. Lanny was ordered to take it, and the others ranged themselves in a circle to hear what was going to be said. Even the bar was forgotten for a time.

"They tell me you are a friend of Hitler's, Mr. Budd." The voice was surprising, that of a child—a sweet little child of ten.

"Yes," replied Lanny meekly. "I have that honor."

"Tell me, does he make a practice of having American friends?"

"I think not, Miss Parsons. So far as I know I am his only American friend."

"And how did that come about?" She didn't add "my little man," but it was exactly so that Lanny had been questioned by duchesses and ambassadors' wives when he was a lad of eight or ten.

The visitor explained, respectfully: "It happened that when I was young, one of my playmates was Kurt Meissner, who grew up to become Germany's most honored Komponist. Another boy at Schloss Stubendorf became one of the Führer's earliest converts and visited him when he was in prison. The Führer never forgets any of those old-timers, and so it came about that I was brought into his circle."

"And tell me, what sort of man is he, really?"

So Lanny was launched upon one of his suave discourses. He put everything he had into it, for he knew that at this moment he was right where he wanted to be. It was for the Hearst newspapers that Louella Parsons wrote her famous column of movie gossip, and she was one of the publisher's intimates and a frequent guest at San Simeon. It wasn't that fate had been so especially kind to Lanny, but that he had been especially careful in figuring where and how to make his Hollywood debut.

———————

HE DIDN'T TELL about his joining the German Army in Dunkirk and being taken back to the Führer's headquarters. He knew that was too much like a Hollywood story, and would discredit the rest of his statements. What he told were the little commonplace things: the Führer's vegetable plate with a poached egg on top, his law against smoking in his home, the fact that you had to appear within two minutes of the sounding of the gong for meals; his fondness for Wagner's music, his insistence that all the women servants and secretaries had to be young Aryan blondes, so different from himself; his fondness for his old Munich companions, such as Herr Kannenberg, the fat little man who had been a *Kellner* and was now Adi's steward, and played the accordion for him in the evening, and sang *"Ach, du lieber Augustin"* and dialect songs from the Inn valley where the son of Alois Schicklgruber had been born. He explained Adi's propaganda technique of choosing a big lie and repeating it incessantly until everybody believed it; he told the story of the Stierwäscher of the Innthal—the peasants who had wanted to enter a white bull in a prize competition, but they had no white bull, so they took a black one and washed it every day for a month and then insisted that it was white, and so they won the prize.

And so on and on, far beyond the limits of confinement to one subject that a cocktail party ordinarily sticks to. There were two men who were on the front page almost every day, and who were very exclusive—Joseph Stalin and Adolf Hitler. There were few in Hollywood who could say they had met either, and probably not one who could say that he had met Hitler within the past half year. Lanny could say it, and prove it by going into details about the scene in the Hotel Crillon, where Hitler had made his headquarters, and the railroad car in the Compiègne forest where the armistice had been signed and Adi had done his little jig dance of triumph. To listen to all this was not merely idle curiosity on the part of Genie's guests, for one of the stock products of Hollywood had become anti-Nazi pictures, and Lanny's intimate stories would be useful to writers, producers, directors, costumers, property men, and on down the line.

PRESENTLY HE WAS telling about Karinhall, which was named after Göring's first wife and was the home of his second. Emmy Sonnemann, having been one of Germany's stage queens, was somebody this audience could understand. Now she had a baby— and that too was becoming a Hollywood custom and a matter of public excitement. Lanny told what happened when you went on a shooting trip with this old-style Teutonic robber baron at his lodge in the Silesian forest called Rominten: how you stood on a high stand while the stags were driven out in front of you, and you picked the one with the best horns and shot him, and then after eating an enormous supper of all kinds of game you put on your overcoat and went out into the moonlit forest where the stags had been laid in the snow, and listened while the trumpeters blew a sort of requiem for the stags, called a Hallali. Surely Hollywood ought to use that some day! And also the pig-sticking in the forests of the Obersalzberg—but those shots might be a bit difficult to get.

Lanny came to the subject of the Reichsmarschall's taste in art, which ran to gentlemen in magnificent costumes and ladies in no costumes at all. For years Lanny had helped him to get rid of paintings he didn't want and to acquire others more to his taste; in passing, the expert remarked: "Just before the war came, Hermann was arranging to purchase a set of sixteenth-century Flemish tapestries from Mr. Hearst's agents in London. He showed me the sketches of them, and told me a story about Sir Neville Henderson, who had inspected the drawings. They were all of nude ladies representing various virtues, and the British Ambassador commented that he didn't see any representing Patience. Göring has a keen sense of humor, and when you hit it he throws his head back and bellows."

At this point the queen of publicity interposed: "Mr. Budd, have you ever met Mr. Hearst?"

"I have never had that pleasure," was the reply. "I missed him on his trip to Paris a couple of years ago."

"He was greatly impressed by both Göring and Hitler."

"So I have been told, and the feeling was reciprocated. Hermann and Adi are both remarkable men, and Mr. Hearst is one who would be able to appreciate them."

"I think he would be interested to hear your account of them."

"I should be honored to meet him, Miss Parsons—and especially if I had your recommendation."

That was all that was said, but after the party broke up the genial Genie remarked: "You made a hit with Louella—and believe me that isn't easy for anybody who monopolizes the conversation!" The hostess was bubbling with satisfaction, for her party had been a success, and she was sure it would get a fat paragraph in the morning. The game of publicity hunting is like the pinball device which you see in drugstores and poolrooms; you invest a lot of money, but it is only rarely that you hit the jackpot.

———————

AT TEN O'CLOCK next morning, after Lanny had finished his bath and his breakfast and his *Los Angeles Examiner*, the telephone rang in his hotel room. "Is this Mr. Lanny Budd? This is Louella Parsons."

"Oh, good morning, Miss Parsons. I have just read what you wrote about me in your column. It is very kind of you indeed."

"I write what I think. If you had been a chatterbox I would have said so—or I wouldn't have said anything."

"Thank you, Miss Parsons."

"I have just talked with Mr. Hearst. He would be pleased if you would visit him. He invites you for lunch today and to spend the week-end at San Simeon."

"But—how can I get there by lunchtime?"

"You will fly. His plane leaves the Burbank airport at eleven-thirty. There will be other passengers, so don't be late."

"I'll do my best, you may be sure."

"You won't need formal clothes; the place is called 'The Ranch.' Bear in mind that all guests are expected in the Great Hall every evening, and all are expected to witness the motion picture show with the Chief. No drinking is permitted in the private rooms."

"I do not drink, Miss Parsons, except when my host expects it."

"Mr. Hearst does not drink, either. There is one more rule that is imperative—no one ever mentions the subject of death in his presence."

"I will bear these admonitions in mind."

"If you do, you will have an enjoyable experience, and if the Chief likes you, you may stay as long as you wish."

"I am most grateful for your kindness, Miss Parsons."

"You may prove your gratitude by giving me any items that are suitable for my column. All my friends do that."

"I shall be truly glad to be enlisted among your friends."

So that was that; Lanny had accomplished his purpose in some thirty-six hours after his car had crossed the borders of the Golden State. He dressed hurriedly, packed his bags, paid his hotel bill, and obtained a map of the Los Angeles district, showing the route to the airport. Lanny was used to getting to places and it caused him no trouble.

He stored his car in a garage near the airport, and as he returned to the building he observed the arrival of a limousine, one of those elaborate custom-built jobs which mark the approach of a potentate, whether political, industrial, or theatrical. With the assistance of a uniformed footman there alighted a small lady with a large amount of blond hair elaborately curled. She wore much paint and powder, the costliest possible furs, and quite a display of jewels: in short, a *tout ensemble* of worldly grandeur. It occurred to Lanny that the lady's face was familiar, but he forbore to stare and went on to the big shiny silver-topped plane.

The lady followed, with the footman carrying her bags, and Lanny perceived that he was to have the honor of traveling with this vision of loveliness. He realized who it must be: the actress whom the lord of San Simeon had installed in his palace something more than two decades ago, and of whom he was accustomed to say that he had spent six million dollars to make her a star. He had set up a producing concern and featured her in several pictures per year, and with the appearance of each picture the Hearst newspapers scattered from Boston to Seattle and from Atlanta to Los Angeles would burst into paeans of praise. In the old days when Lanny had hobnobbed with newspapermen at international conferences, this procedure had been a theme for cynical jesting, and to a young Pink it had seemed a measure of his country's social decay.

Lanny gave his name to the pilot of the plane, who had it on a list. The lady said: "I am Marion Davies," and the guest replied: "I am indeed honored, Miss Davies; I am one of your ardent fans." This was a measure of Lanny's social decay, for his true opinion was that she couldn't act and that her efforts were pathetic.

The roar of the plane made conversation difficult, so Lanny surveyed the landscape of California from the point of view of an eagle. First, masses of tumbled mountains, some bare and rocky, others with vegetation dried brown at this season of the year; then valleys with farms and orchards, and gray threads that were roads; always, off to the left, the blue Pacific, with a line of white surf, and now and then a vessel large or small. Very few towns, and rivers mostly dry beds; a land of which vast tracts were kept for grazing by wealthy owners who didn't want settlers and money so much as they wanted space and fresh air. Only a land-values tax could have reached them, and there could be no such tax because they owned the newspapers and controlled both political machines.

The trip took about an hour, which meant a couple of hundred miles. A great stretch of lonely land, and then, close to the sea, La Cuesta Encantada—the enchanted hill—and on it a group of elaborate buildings which might have been the summer palace of the prince of the Asturias. The plane came down to a private airport, and there was a car to take them to the houses, and a station wagon for their bags. "Are you familiar with California, Mr. Budd?" inquired the lady; her real name was Douras, and she had been born in Brooklyn, two facts to which you did not refer.

Lanny replied: "It is my first visit, and I am agape with wonder." It was the proper attitude. "I have lived most of my life abroad," he continued. He had this *grande dame* of the silver screen to himself for a few minutes, and knew that the success of his enterprise might depend upon the impression he made. "So I have got most of my knowledge of America from your pictures and others. Now, when I see these landscapes I think I am on location, and when I meet Miss Marion Davies face to face I think I am back in Little Old New York—or I am with Polly of the Circus, or Blondie of the Follies, or Peg O' My Heart."

"Dear me, you really must be one of my fans!" exclaimed the actress, who wasn't acting much nowadays, because in her forties she could no longer play juvenile parts and nobody dared to suggest any other parts.

"It must be a wonderful thing to know that you have given so much pleasure to so many millions of people, Miss Davies. Unless my memory fails me I saw *When Knighthood Was in Flower* in a tiny village called Stubendorf in Upper Silesia, and I saw *Miss Glory* in a wretched old shed called a theater in Southern Spain. I have never forgotten how the audience wept." The treacherous one made these speeches with tender feeling, and knew from the way they were received that he had made a friend at court. He had known what he was coming to California for, and he had not failed to stop in a library and look up in *Who's Who* the name of William Randolph Hearst, and that of his leading lady friend, with the list of her "starring vehicles."

———————

THE SON OF Budd-Erling had traveled three thousand miles, and here was his destination, the fabulous San Simeon, called "The Ranch." It was the ranch to end all ranchos, covering four hundred and twenty square miles, which meant that from the mansion you could ride some fifteen miles in any direction, except out to sea, and never leave the estate. You could ride a horse, as "Willie" had done all through his boyhood; or if your taste ran to the eccentric, you could ride a zebra, or a llama, or a giraffe, a bison or yak or elephant or kangaroo or emu or cassowary. There were herds of all these creatures on the place, and numbers of central California cowboys to take care of them, and if a guest expressed a desire to ride one, the cowboys would no doubt take it as a perfectly normal eccentricity of these Hollywood folk. There were also lions and tigers and pumas and leopards in cages, and if Lanny had announced that he was a tamer of wild beasts and wanted to practice on these, the host would no doubt have seen to arranging it.

But the P.A. was a tamer of a more dangerous kind of wild beast; those who killed not for food but for glory; who killed not merely men but nations and civilizations. He was driven to La Casa del Sol—all the elaborate guest houses had Spanish names, as did everything else on the ranch. He was escorted to an elegant suite with a bathroom whose walls and floor and sunken tub were all of marble. He took a glance into one of the ample closets, and discovered therein complete outfits of every sort—one side of the closet for men and the other for women—pajamas, dressing gowns, swimming costumes, tennis and golf and riding clothes, and evening clothes which were permissible though not required. Lanny didn't stop to find out how they would fit him; the sun was shining and it was warm, so he put on his own palm beach suit and, following orders, made his way to La Casa Grande, which is Spanish for what on Southern plantations is "the big house." It was an immense structure in the style of an old Spanish mission; underneath it, the visitor learned before long, were acres of storerooms packed with art treasures like those he had inspected in the Bronx.

Here came the master of these treasures, the creator of this *Arabian Nights'* dream of magnificence. He had been tall and large in proportion, like most men of these wide-open spaces, but now his shoulders were bowed and there were signs of a paunch. He had a long face and an especially long nose; his enemies called it a horse face and had made it familiar in cartoons. His strangest feature was a pair of small eyes, watery blue, so pale that they seemed lifeless: no feeling in them at all, and very little in the face, or in the flabby, unresponsive hand. A man withdrawn, a man who never gave himself; now a man grown old, with pouches under his eyes, sagging cheeks, and wattles under his chin. Lanny thought: a man unhappy, not pleased with the people around him, not pleased with his memories, and with no hopes for this world or the next.

It was easy to imagine things about him. Was his reason for keeping so many people around him the fact that he could avoid observing the defects of any one? There were seldom fewer than fifty guests, Lanny had been told, and this week-end he estimated there were seventy-five; he had to meet them all—there was an efficient major-domo who took him the rounds. There were faces familiar from the screen, and others whose names told him that they were top executives, producers and directors of pictures. He guessed that they were the friends of Marion Davies rather than of Hearst, who had drifted into her world, the world of make-believe, after he had failed so desolately to make a success in the world of politics and public affairs. He had tried to help the people—or so he must have told himself—but they had refused to trust him. Here was a new world, easier to live in; one made to order, and in which wealth could have its way.

The important, the big-money people of "the industry"—so it called itself—came here and made the place a sort of country club without dues. There was everything you could think of in the way of convenience; a Midas expended fifteen million dollars a year to maintain it, and granted the use of it to his courtiers and favorites. There was a bar, never closed, and you could have anything you asked for, provided you drank it in the public rooms. There was an immense medieval hall where you could play pool or billiards or pingpong, in between thousand-year-old choir stalls—incongruous, but no more so than other features of this fantastic estate. You could hunt or fish, or play tennis in courts with gold-quartz walls; you could swim in a pool of fresh cold water, or in another of salt water pumped up from the ocean and warmed.

II

AFTER THE COCKTAIL HOUR, the lord of the manor took the arm of his star of the first magnitude and led a sort of grand-opera march into the dining-hall, which was in the style of a medium-sized cathedral. Everything was supposed to be different from what it was, and this apparently was a monks' refectory; there was no cloth on the long table, which was of bare heavy wood, many centuries old. Priceless old china and glassware suggested a museum, printed menus suggested a hotel dining-room, while paper napkins suggested the lunch counter of a "five and ten." The center of the table was marked by a long line of condiments and preserves, all in their original containers; all homemade, and the host was very proud of them. Like nothing else the much-traveled Lanny had seen on this earth was the entourage of Miss Marion Davies during the repast. Behind her chair stood a liveried man-servant holding an embroidered silk tray with her toilet articles, and at a sign he would step forward and she would make use of them. The chair beside her was occupied by an elderly dog whose name was Gandhi—even though he was not a vegetarian; as each course of the elaborate meal was served, a special attendant brought Gandhi a silver tray with slices of choice meats, which were eaten with due propriety.

After the meal came the motion-picture showing, in a projection room built for that purpose. Attendance was obligatory upon all guests, and Lanny wondered about this; he had had no such experience since he had been a pupil at St. Thomas's Academy in Connecticut and had been obliged to attend chapel every morning. Was it the host's purpose to dignify the motion-picture art by setting it on the level of a form of worship? Was it a means of doing honor to the gracious lady who deigned to occupy the "Celestial Suite" in his palace? (Mrs. William Randolph Hearst lived in a mansion in New York.) Could it possibly have happened that in times past some guest had had the atrocious taste to wish to read his evening paper while a picture of Miss Davies was being run? The lord of this manor was a person of whims and furious temper; if an employee displeased him he would kick him out without ceremony and never see him again. Lanny had never forgotten a story told to him by one of the Hearst correspondents abroad: the man had been called to a conference in the master's New York home, and they had talked until long after midnight; the host, being hungry, had taken his guest to the icebox; finding it locked, he had not let himself be balked, but had taken a red-painted fire axe from the wall and chopped his way through the door.

The "feature" for this Saturday night was one of those comedies which had come to be known as "screwball." It had not yet been released, for of course this master of infinite publicity had the right to priority, and would never risk showing his guests anything shopworn. The picture had been made for a public which found life dull and depressing, and which paid its money for one purpose, to get as far away from reality as possible. The heroine of the story was the daughter of a millionaire who lived in a house with the customary drawing-room resembling a railroad station, and the hero was a handsome male doll supposed to be a newspaper reporter, that being an occupation which made it plausible for him to encounter a millionaire's daughter. The young lady, wearing a different expensive costume in every scene, tried to run away from a traffic cop and landed in jail under an alias; the reporter tried to get her out, and there resulted a series of absurd adventures, most of which all motion-picture people had seen and helped to produce in many previous films.

In short, it was a stereotype, as much so as the faces and gestures of the leading man and lady. The reporter was supposed to be poor, but when you visited his mother's home you discovered that it had a kitchen half as big as a railroad station, and that the mother and sisters wore the smartest clothes and had their hair waved and not a single strand out of place—otherwise the scene would have been reshot. Lanny watched the episodes, some of which depended upon what Broadway called wisecracks, and others upon slapstick, people falling on their behinds or into a fishpond; the scenes whirled by at breathless pace, as if the producers were driven by fear that if they paused for a moment the public might have time to realize what vapidity was being fed to them.

Lanny couldn't make his escape; he had to stick it out. But there were no chains on his mind; he thought about these men and women, all persons of importance, of some kind of responsibility. What were *their* thoughts while they watched this entertainment? In their own word, it was "tripe," and to the last person they must have been aware of the fact. Somebody here had produced it for the purpose of making money; and the others would be thinking: How much will it gross? They would speculate: Is there anything I can learn from it, any ideas I can take over, any actors, any writers I might hire?

Lanny knew the formula by which they excused themselves: it was "what the public wants." The public, in the view of movie magnates, had no heart, no conscience, no brains; the public didn't want to learn anything, it didn't want to think, it didn't want to improve itself, or to see its children better than itself. It just wanted to be amused, on its lowest level; it wanted to see life made ridiculous by grotesque mishaps; it wanted to revel in wealth, regardless of how it was gained or how wasted; above all it wanted to watch adolescents pairing off, kissing and getting ready to get married—boy meets girl! The assumption was that they would live happy ever after, though never was it shown how that miracle would be achieved, and though the divorce rate in America was continually increasing.

This code expressed boundless cynicism concerning human nature, an unfaith become a faith. It was contempt fanned by the fires of greed; it was treason to the soul of man erected into a business system, organized, systematized, and spread into every corner of the earth. This particular "hunk of cheese"—one of the phrases Lanny had learned on the previous evening—was being offered to a world tottering upon the edge of an abyss. While it was being previewed, London Bridge might be falling down, and the British Empire crashing to its doom; before the picture had finished its run, America itself might be fighting for its life; but the mob would still guffaw at a "dame" being slapped on her "butt."

Lanny thought it was no accident that Hearst had sought refuge in this screen world; his personality and his life had been an incarnation of the same treason to the soul of man. For more than half a century his papers had been feeding scandal and murder to the American public; he had been setting psychological traps for their pennies and nickels, and because these traps succeeded, his contempt for the victims had been confirmed. By such means he had accumulated the second greatest fortune in America, and when he had got it he didn't know what to do with it, except to build this caricature of a home, this costliest junk yard on the earth. Here it was, and he had invited a swarm of courtiers and sycophants, and entertained them by presenting them with a caricature of themselves, a world as empty and false as San Simeon itself. The most incredible fact of all—so thought the presidential agent—he *made* them look at it! He rubbed their noses in their own vomit! Did he hate them that much?

III

THE HOST HAD BEEN told about his new guest, and after the showing invited him to view some of the special treasures in this home. Thus Lanny learned a new aspect of this strange individual; he really loved beautiful things. Not the men who produced them— during his stay in San Simeon Lanny didn't meet a single artist, and he saw very few *objets d'art* produced by living persons. What Hearst loved were the objects, as things to admire, to show, and above all, to possess. He unlocked a special cabinet and took out a rare vase of Venetian glass; it was something marvelous, a rich green fading into the color of milk, cloudy, translucent, and when you held it up to the light the colors wavered and pulsed as if the object were alive. "When you have something like that," remarked the Duce of San Simeon, "you have a pleasure that endures; you come to think of it as a friend."

"Ah, yes," replied the expert, who had learned something about the human heart as well as the price of paintings. "And it does not turn out to be something other than you had thought. It does not become corrupted; it does not betray you or slander you; it does not try to get anything out of you."

Was there a flash of light in those pale blank eyes, or was it just a reflection from the shiny surface of the vase? "I see you understand the meaning of art, Mr. Budd," remarked the host.

They wandered through the halls of this private museum, and Lanny hadn't needed any advance preparation. He knew these painters and their works, and could tell interesting stories about both; he could make technical comments that were right; and most important of all, he knew values. He was used to talking to men who lived by and for money, and here was one of the world's greatest money masters, a man who had bought not merely all kinds of things but men and women for a vast array of purposes. When he had come to New York, half a century ago, to shoulder his way into metropolitan journalism, he had bought most of Pulitzer's crack staff; he had even hired a room in the World Building so as to do it with speed and convenience. He had bought editors, writers, advertising and circulation men, all by the simple process of finding out what they were getting and offering them twice as much. And he had the same attitude toward paintings; when he wanted one he got it, regardless of price—but he remembered the price!

So now Lanny remarked: "I found a Goya rather like that four years ago, while I was running away from the war in Spain, and I sold it in Pittsburgh for twenty-five thousand dollars." The host replied: "I got that one for seventeen thousand, but it was a long time ago." And then Lanny: "It is a fine specimen; it might bring thirty or forty thousand now. The well-to-do have discovered that old masters are a form of sound investment, and offer the advantage that you don't have to pay duty."

Presently they were in front of a Canaletto, a glimpse of Venice, bright and clear like the tones of a small bell. Lanny remarked: "I sold one for Hermann Göring not long ago."

It was a bait, and was grabbed instantly. "Louella tells me you know Göring well, and also Hitler."

"I have had that good fortune. I have known the Führer for some thirteen years, and Hermann for half that."

"They are extraordinary men," said the host. "I should like to talk with you about them sometime while you are here."

"With pleasure, Mr. Hearst." It was a date.

IV

IN THE MIDDLE OF Sunday morning, while the guests sallied forth to amuse themselves on the estate, or sat on the veranda in the sunshine reading copies of the *Examiner* which had been flown in by plane, the publisher invited his new friend into the study where no one came save by invitation. There Lanny spread before him a treasure of knowledge concerning Nazi-Fascism which he had been accumulating over a period of two decades. He told how he had first seen Mussolini, then a journalist, in a *trattoria* in San Remo, in a furious argument with his former Red associates; how later, in Cannes, he had interviewed him during an international conference. He told about Schloss Stubendorf, where he had visited Kurt Meissner as a boy, and about Heinrich Jung who had become one of the earliest of the Nazis, and had taken Lanny to Adi's apartment in Berlin in the days before the Führer had had that or any other title.

"I thought I was something of a Pink in those days," Lanny said, "and Hitler had a program very much like the one you had when you were young, Mr. Hearst. He was going to put an end to interest slavery, as he called it, and 'bust the trusts'; it sounded like one of Brisbane's editorials with all the important phrases in caps."

"That was a long time ago," remarked the publisher, with perhaps a trace of nostalgia. "We have all learned that the trusts can be made useful with proper regulation."

"Of course; but the program pleased the people, in Berlin and Munich as it had in New York and Chicago. It is a fact which I have pointed out to my friends in England and France that the Nazis did not come into power as a movement to put down the Reds and to preserve large-scale business enterprise; they came as a radical movement, offering the people what they thought was a constructive program. It very much resembled the old Populist program in this country."

"You are correct," said Mr. Hearst. "But the trouble is, Roosevelt has stolen all our thunder, and what can we do?"

"Congressman Fish asked the same question when I mentioned the subject to him. I cannot answer, because my specialty is painting, not statesmanship. All I can do is to point out the facts I have observed. In countries where the people have the ballot you have to promise them something desirable, otherwise the opposition will outbid you."

"They are raising the price higher and higher, Mr. Budd. I have long been saying that if the bidding continues, it will result in the destruction of our democratic system."

"You may be right. There are many in England who observe labor's demands continually increasing, and who look with envy upon what Hitler has been able to achieve."

"But even he has to go on making promises, Mr. Budd."

"Of course; but he is able to put off the fulfillment until after victory is won. Then, in all probability, he will find it possible to keep the promises. The Germans will be a ruling race, and all others on the Continent will work for them; so it should be possible to give German workers a larger share of the product."

"You think he is certain to win?"

"How is it possible to think otherwise? He no longer has any opponent but Britain; and can Britain conquer the Continent of Europe? Sooner or later their resources will give out, and they will have to accept the compromise which Hitler holds out to them. I can tell you about this, because I myself have been the bearer of messages from the Führer to Lord Wickthorpe, who has just resigned his post at the Foreign Office in protest against Churchill's stubbornness."

V

NATURALLY, THE PUBLISHER of eighteen newspapers wanted to know all about this mission. He wanted to know what the proposals were and what chance there would be of modifying them. He wanted to know what terms had been offered to the French, and what secret clauses might be in the armistice agreement with France. He wanted to hear about the struggle going on between Laval and Pétain within the Vichy Government, and how that was likely to turn out. Was Hitler going to get the French Fleet, and was he strong enough to take Gibraltar? What was the actual strength of the Italian army, and would it be able to break into Egypt and close the Suez Canal? An extraordinarily complicated war, and fascinating if you could take an aloof position, and not be worried about the possibility of your own country being drawn into it!

A year or so after the Nazis had taken power, William Randolph Hearst had paid a visit to both Rome and Berlin. He had made a deal with the Nazis whereby his International News Service was to have the exclusive use of all Nazi official news—a very good thing financially. The publisher had had several confidential talks with the Führer, and told Lanny how greatly he had been impressed by this man's grasp of international affairs. "Naturally, I am sympathetic to his domestic program," he explained. "There can be no question that he has made Germany over, and that he has been a blessing to the country. But I could not continue to endorse him, because of what he has done to the Jews. You understand that—if only for business reasons."

"Certainly," replied Lanny with a smile. "New York appears to have become a Jewish city."

Six years had passed since Mr. Hearst's visit; and what had these years done to the Führer, and to his *Nummer Zwei* and his *Nummer Drei?* The host plied his guest with questions, and the guest answered frankly, telling many stories about the Führer's home life, both at Berchtesgaden and Berlin; about Göring's hunting lodge in the Schorfheide, which had been the property of the Prussian State, but Göring had calmly taken it over and built it into a palace, much on the order of San Simeon, though Lanny forbore to mention that. He talked about Hess's interest in astrologers and spirit mediums, that being no secret in regard to the head of the Nazi Party. He told of confidential talks with these men, and explained how it was possible for them to accept an American art expert as a friend and even an adviser. There had to be somebody to take messages to other countries and bring replies, and official personalities were often unsatisfactory because they had become involved in factional strife and intrigues at home.

"Göring hates Ribbentrop like poison, and so does Hess," Lanny explained, "and all three of them hate Goebbels. The Führer uses them all, and plays one against another; he 'never trusts anyone completely, except possibly Hess, and when I come along he may be relieved to meet somebody who is untouched by this steam of jealousy and suspicion. He feels that he has known me from boyhood, because of my intimacy with Kurt Meissner and Heinrich Jung, two men who have been his loyal followers from the beginning and who have never once asked a favor of him. Then, too, both the Führer and Göring have more than once offered me money, and I have refused it, which impresses them greatly."

"They wanted you in their service?"

"Yes; but I explained to them that if I incurred such obligations I should part with my sense of freedom; I should begin to worry about whether or not I was earning my keep, and they would begin to think I was an idler, and would start making demands upon me."

A smile came upon the long face of this man of so many millions. "Are you telling me this so that I won't make you a proposal, Mr. Budd?"

"No, it hadn't occurred to me that you might wish to."

"You are a modest man, indeed. What you have been telling me is of importance to one who is getting on in years and inclined to stay in his own chimney corner. Firsthand information is not easy to come by, and I would be very pleased to pay for it, and would promise never to put the least pressure upon you. If you would come to see me now and then and let me pump your mind as I have just been doing, it would be worth, say, fifty thousand dollars a year to me — or more, if that would help."

"I have always heard that you were munificent, Mr. Hearst, and now you are proving it. I would be glad to be numbered among your friends, and now and then to run out and see you; but I would rather do it as I do for other friends, because of the pleasure I get from being helpful. My profession of art expert provides for my needs, and I am one of those fortunate persons whose work is play."

"You are able to earn so much?"

"I don't need so much, because I am a guest wherever I go — at my father's home in Connecticut, at my mother's home on the Riviera, at my former wife's home in England. It sounds odd, so I must explain that Lord Wickthorpe married Irma Barnes, and we have managed to remain friends. I have a little daughter who lives at Wickthorpe Castle, and I go there to stay with her. It is a box seat from which to view the affairs of the British Empire."

The man of money was troubled by this attitude toward his own divinity, which was money. Quite possibly nothing of the sort had ever happened to him before. "You do not consider the necessity of providing for your old age?"

"There, too, I have been favored by fortune. My father has considerable money, and if I should reach old age, I have reason to expect to inherit a share of it."

That put the matter on a different basis; it established this suave gentleman among the small group of social equals. "I suppose I have to accept your decision, Mr. Budd; but bear me in mind on your travels, and any time you have information or advice which you think I ought to have, send it to me by cable, and if you will let me have the name of your bank in this country, I will see that the cost is deposited to your account."

"As you know, Mr. Hearst, the British government makes cabling a dubious matter in wartime. But when I am in this country I can telegraph you—and it does sometimes happen that I have a suggestion that might be of interest."

"Dictate it to a stenographer and send it collect," commanded the Duce of San Simeon. "Don't worry about the length—you have carte blanche from this time forth."

VI

LOUELLA PARSONS HAD told Lanny that he might be invited to stay as long as he pleased, and so it turned out. He accepted, because he was curious about this man of vast power whom he regarded as one of the fountainheads of American Fascism; also about the guests who came and went so freely at this free country club. They were the rulers of California; the officials, the judges, the newspaper managers and editors, the big businessmen; but above all the motion-picture colony in its higher departments, the masters of super-publicity.

The oddest business in the world, it seemed to the son of Budd-Erling; the providing of dreams to all the peoples of the earth. "The industry" was about as old as Lanny himself, and the men in it had grown up with it, and didn't find it so strange. Its big businessmen were very little different from those who provided clothing in New York and other cities; there, too, the fashions had to be studied; elegance was another kind of dream, and the public's whims could make or break you. The men who manufactured and marketed entertainment bought the services of other men and women, just as a newspaper publisher did, and they estimated the value of these persons by what could be made out of their talents.

If a man wrote a best-selling novel they would hire him to write for them at several thousand dollars a week, and would install him in a cubicle with a typewriter and a secretary; if they had nothing for him to do at the moment they would expect him to wait, and they might forget him for six months, but they saw no reason why he should object, so long as he was receiving his salary check. His best-seller might have had to do with, say, the sufferings of the sharecroppers of Louisiana, and they would put him to work on a script having to do with a murder mystery in Hawaii. You might hear half a dozen anecdotes similar to this in a morning's chat at San Simeon, but you weren't supposed to laugh—a polite little smile would answer all purposes.

Just now the presidential campaign was at its climax, and much of the conversation of the guests had to do with this subject. "That Man in the White House" was trying to grab off a third term, and most of the top men in "the industry," like the top men in all the other industries, considered that the salvation of the country depended upon the rebuking of this insolent ambition. Every morning the *Examiner* came, and every afternoon the *Herald-Express*, Hearst papers filled with editorials and columns and doctored news, all in a frenzied effort to discredit the Administration. The guests read these papers, and talked in the same vein. Lanny heard nobody dissenting; the nearest any came to it were two or three who suggested mildly that the affairs of the country would go on much the same whether it was Willkie or Roosevelt. These men were looked upon as in very bad taste, and Lanny kept carefully away from them.

VII

EVERY DAY AT San Simeon there arrived by airmail copies of eighteen Hearst newspapers from all over America. Presumably one man couldn't read them all, but he could glance over them with a pair of eyes practiced for more than half a century; then he would dictate a telegram to the managing editor of each paper, saying what was wrong, and the telegrams were famous for their vigorous language. This had been the practice ever since 1887, when Willie Hearst had taken over his daddy's newspaper, the *San Francisco Examiner*—soon after being expelled from Harvard University for the offense of sending to each of his professors an elegant *pot de chambre* with the professor's name inscribed in gold letters on the inside.

Now and then this grown-up playboy would retire from the company of his guests and seat himself in a corner of the Great Hall, and resting a pad of paper on the arm of his chair would start writing with a lead pencil. Nobody disturbed him at such times, for they knew that he was writing a directive which would change the policy of his papers, or perhaps an editorial which would change the policy of the United States government. Sometimes these editorials would be signed with their author's name, and in that case they would appear double-column in large type; or they might be published as run-of-the-mine editorials, always in all the papers on the same day.

It was quite a pulpit, and if you knew the text you could pretty well write the sermon yourself. Willie Hearst had hated the British Empire ever since he had shot off his first firecracker on the Fourth of July. He had hated France ever since the year 1930, when he had been ordered out of that country after having brought all the guests of San Simeon for a tour of Europe on a whim. He hated the Reds and the Pinks, every variety of them, ever since they had undertaken to carry out the program which Willie had been advocating when he hoped to become the people's candidate. He hated F.D.R. for having succeeded where Willie had failed—and especially for having promoted an income tax which had made it necessary for Willie to part with his art treasures and with the financial management of his chain of publications.

Lanny watched closely, day by day, and was quite sure that he recognized where some of his host's editorials had come from. For a secret agent not merely had to listen, he had to voice ideas, and be sure that the ideas were those his listener wanted to hear. Afterwards he winced when he discovered these ideas being circulated to the extent of five million copies, sometimes in the very words he had used. This new Willie-Lanny team told the American people: "If the American people want war, they should surely re-elect Mr. Roosevelt. Whether they want it or not, they will surely get it by electing him."

And again: "Congress, in the gravest hour in the history of the Republic, has ceased to function constitutionally. It is not asked whether it wants war or peace. The people, the ultimate power in our democracy, are treated and shushed away from official doors in Washington—doors behind which we are being sold down the river to war and economic slavery."

And yet again: "By its pernicious system of political bounties and pillage of the public treasury, and by its vicious appeals to class-consciousness—which inevitably begets class hatred—the New Deal has actually labored to make America mob-minded, and neither law nor democracy can survive in a mob-minded country."

VIII

ELECTION DAY, November 5, 1940, arrived, and there were few guests at San Simeon, because they considered it their duty to scatter to their homes and record their votes against the great American Dictator. But after voting they came by planeload and by motorcar to play tennis and ride horseback and swim until it was time to turn on the radio in the Great Hall and listen to the returns. California, being three hours behind the East, gets the early returns in the latter part of the afternoon; by five o'clock they were coming in a flood, and by dinnertime it was all over, and everybody knew that the Third Term had swept the country. Willkie was going to carry only ten states—and you could get what comfort there was in the fact that it was a gain of eight over what the Republican candidate of four years ago had managed to obtain.

Lanny could not recall when he had ever seen so large a collection of unhappy human beings—certainly not since he had been in the old gray smoke-stained building in Downing Street, the home of the British Foreign Office, on the night or rather the early morning when Hitler had begun his raid on Poland. Conversation in the San Simeon refectory was in low tones, and not much of it. Lanny wondered: Was this Hollywood play-acting, carried on for the benefit of the host, or had they actually come to believe their own propaganda? Anyhow, it was like a funeral repast, and to have laughed would have been a shocking breach of taste.

Later in the evening, in the host's very private study, the P. A. had the serious talk for which he had journeyed across a continent. "We have met with a grave disappointment, Mr. Hearst," began the guest, "and before I take my leave, I should like to know what you think about it, and what I should advise my friends abroad."

What Mr. Hearst thought was that the country was in one hell of a mess, but there was nothing that he or anybody else could do about it. The American people had made their bed and would have to lie in it; they had lighted a hot fire under themselves and would now stew in their own juice. The vexed old man predicted a series of calamities, to which getting into the war was but the vestibule. The public debt would pile up and there would be no way out but to declare national bankruptcy; the industry of the country would be converted to war purposes, and likewise its labor, and when the horror was over, whichever side won would be the loser. There would be such an unemployment problem as had never been dreamed of in the world; there would be strikes, riots, and insurrections. Worst of all, there would be the Red Dictator sitting in the Kremlin, chortling with glee; he would be piling up his military equipment, and at the end he would be the only power left in Europe; he wouldn't even have to take possession by force of arms, his Communist agents would do it by propaganda, and bankrupt countries would tumble into his lap like so many ripe peaches.

Lanny waited until this Book of Lamentations had arrived at a chapter end, and then he said: "I agree with every word you have spoken, Mr. Hearst. My father has been saying the same things ever since Munich. I think the greater number of our responsible businessmen realize the dangers, and there are some I have talked with who aren't disposed to sit by and let fate have its way."

"But what can they do?"

"We Americans have hypnotized ourselves with the idea of the sovereignty of the ballot; and that is a great convenience to our opponents, who have the mob on their side. As you well know, it is the property owners who are going to have to pay when this debacle comes, because they are the only ones who have anything to pay with."

"No doubt about that, Budd." Lanny was being promoted by the dropping of the "Mister."

"Well, Hitler showed the industrialists of Germany that they didn't have to lie down and submit to having their pockets emptied; and it seems to some men I know that they have the same elemental right of self-defense."

"You mean they are proposing to turn Roosevelt out? That would mean a civil war. I couldn't face it!"

"It might mean a small-sized one, but surely it would be cheaper than the one we are being betrayed into. Just think of it, we are being invited to conquer the Continent of Europe! We are being put into the position where we shall be obliged to do it, for Germany will not submit forever to the treacherous underground war that Roosevelt is conducting. Also, Japan will not sit by in idleness, and we shall find that we have undertaken to conquer Asia too."

"All that is beyond dispute, Budd. But, good God, we haven't the means for overthrowing the Administration!"

"There are some who think we can get the means; and it is a matter of no little importance to them to know what your attitude will be."

The Duce of San Simeon did not exclaim: "Get out of my house, you scoundrel!" Instead he remarked, rather sadly: "I am an old man, and such adventures must be left to younger spirits."

"Old men for counsel, young men for war, the proverb says. The question is, what counsel you have to give. Surely this cannot be the first time you have heard the idea!"

"I have heard it talked about a lot, naturally. But if any group is contemplating action, I have not been informed of it."

"If tonight's news does not bring them to the point of action, then they might as well stop talking. Roosevelt is going to take this election as a complete endorsement, and will go ahead with his plans more recklessly than ever."

"That we can be sure of, Budd."

"If there are men who mean to act, they will want support, financial as well as moral. Understand, please, I wouldn't touch any money myself; but I might put them in contact with you if you would permit it."

The Duce of San Simeon looked worried; as much so as he had looked in a photograph which Lanny had seen of him when his newspapers had charged four senators with having accepted bribes, and then, summoned before an investigating committee, he had watched the documents in the case proved to be forgeries. Said W.R.H.: "This is a matter in which one could not afford even to be named without careful consideration. I shall have to ask that you do not mention me to anyone without first telling me who the person is and giving me an opportunity to consent or refuse. Count me out of it!"

"That is a proper request, Mr. Hearst, and I assure you that you may rely absolutely upon my discretion."

"It is a matter that I cannot leave to anyone's discretion. You must agree positively not to mention me in connection with this matter. *It is far too serious.*"

"You have that word. But let me urge this upon you in the meantime: Do not weaken in your opposition to Roosevelt and his war policies."

"That you may count upon, on my word. The Hearst papers will stand like a rock in the midst of a raging torrent."

So they left the matter. It wasn't until next morning that Lanny discovered how this man of much forethought had prepared in advance and sent to his newspapers an editorial to be published in the event that his long-maintained verbal war upon the Presidential Dictatorship should turn out to be unsuccessful. Said the *Los Angeles Examiner,* on the morning after the election: "The Hearst newspapers have never questioned the right of the American people to give Mr. Roosevelt a third term, or any number of terms he may seek and they see fit to grant."

Four

"How I Ended Poverty in California": The EPIC Movement

Retiring from political life in 1934, Upton Sinclair now lives the life of a recluse in Monrovia, perennially engaged in writing the Lanny Budd novels. A remarkable man, this Upton Sinclair. During the EPIC campaign, I interviewed him one insufferably hot August afternoon with a brush fire burning furiously in the hills back of Pasadena...While he failed to convince me that the EPIC plan was feasible, he thoroughly convinced me that poverty and want could be banished from the earth.
—*Carey McWilliams, "The Politics of Utopia," 1946*

CALIFORNIA WAS NOT shielded from the economic disaster that created the Great Depression. Some of the state's chief products— specialty crops, tourism, and movies—made California particularly vulnerable to the contraction of national income after 1929. Agricultural revenues plunged by $400 million between 1929 and 1932; rural areas were poverty stricken; developers and real estate firms crumbled, "revealing a sad picture of fraud, embezzlement, and other forms of financial chicanery that spelled ruin for thousands."[1] Sinclair was a Socialist all his life, but the situation in California was so desperate that he chose to run for governor as a Democrat. He called his program EPIC, the acronym for End Poverty in California. A group of Democrats in Santa Monica led by Gilbert Stevenson, former owner of the landmark Miramar Hotel, had persuaded Sinclair that he might be able to win as a Democrat; if he won the primary, he would face the unpopular Republican governor Frank Merriam.

In June 1934, Will Rogers told his readers that the famous author Upton Sinclair was running for governor of California: "a darn nice fellow, and just plum smart, and if he could deliver even some of the things he promises should not only be governor of one state, but president of all of 'em."[2] After the primary, Webb Waldron, correspondent for *Today* magazine, drove across the curving Arroyo Seco Bridge into Pasadena to interview the candidate. He described Sinclair's house as "a rather shabby jerry-built structure in a modest workingman's neighborhood." He reported that when he knocked:

> Sinclair, a spry fellow about five feet seven inches tall, greeted his visitor in pajamas and bathrobe...Despite weeks of campaigning and a long night studying election returns, his face showed only faint lines of fatigue, and he answered one question after another, sharply, concisely, and soothingly. His words rang with urgency but his voice was soft, his manner boyish, charming, bemused.[3]

William Randolph Hearst was in Germany visiting with Mussolini and Hitler when he learned that Sinclair had swept the Democratic primary. As Greg Mitchell describes it:

> Up and down the state, terrified Republicans and outraged Democrats faced a nightmare of their own making. Earl Warren in Oakland, A. P. Giannini in San Francisco, Herbert Hoover in Palo Alto, Harry Chandler in Los Angeles, Irving Thalberg in Hollywood—they all knew they could no longer sit back and let California be captured by the muckraking author, militant vegetarian, erstwhile Socialist, scourge of the ruling class, and now Democratic nominee for governor, Upton Sinclair.[4]

The *Los Angeles Times*'s Chandler held a war council with members of the city's chamber of commerce. They hired the advertising firm of Lord and Thomas, the first time an ad agency was used in an electoral campaign. MGM Studios created fake newsreels featuring actors paid to excoriate Sinclair, while the *Los Angeles Times*, the *Oakland Tribune,* and the *San Francisco Chronicle* "organized a media blitz to discredit EPIC in every way possible."[5] *Times* political writer Kyle Palmer was loaned to movie czar Will Hays to organize the movie industry's participation in the campaign. Studio workers were assessed one day's wages to pay for the newsreels which theater owners were forced to show.

Sinclair's supporters fought back by loudly objecting when the newsreels were aired in theaters, and even Chandler's agents ended up befriending Sinclair. Ed Ainsworth, a hatchet man for the *Times,* had the job of selecting quotes from Sinclair's novels and placing them, out of context, in large black boxes on the front page. Kate Ainsworth recalls, "Every conservative Republican hated Sinclair's guts. But my husband was dissolved by his personality and little jokes."[6]

Hollywood plunged full-tilt into politics. Democrats James Cagney, Melvyn Douglas, and Frederick March railed against MGM's anti-Sinclair smear tactics.[7] Five days before the election, Aimee Semple McPherson, notorious evangelist, strode like an "avenging angel, dressed all in white" into an anti-Sinclair rally at Shrine Auditorium, dramatically lowering the American flag and raising the Russian flag. "Do we want that Red flag?" she inquired. "Do we want it with all that it means—intolerance, atheism, licentiousness, rebellion, annihilation, anarchism?" Shouting to wild approval, she pulled down the Red flag, raised the Stars and Stripes, and shouted, "We will pour out our votes to maintain its integrity!"[8] When the pageant ended, Jean Harlow, Clark Gable, and Norma Shearer all sent floral arrangements to the stage.

In the days before the election, nine thousand people jammed the Civic Auditorium in Pasadena to hear Upton Sinclair. Organizers turned away six thousand more, so Sinclair came out to speak to them from the front steps. He explained that he had argued for twenty-five years with H. L. Mencken "about the wisdom and the true nature of 'the people': I have been Mencken's prize boob because I believed in you. Now, we shall find out which of us is right."[9]

Notes:

1. Richard Rice, William Bullough, and Richard Orsi, *The Elusive Eden* (New York: McGraw Hill, 2002), 424

2. James M. Smallwood, ed., *Will Rogers' Weekly Articles* VI (Stillwater, Okla.: Oklahoma State University Press, 1980–1982)

3. Webb Waldron, *Today*, October 6, 1934

4. Greg Mitchell, *The Campaign of the Century* (New York: Random House, 1992), 3, 4

5. Robert Gottlieb and Irene Wolt, *Thinking Big: The Story of the* Los Angeles Times, *Its Publishers, and Their Influence on Southern California* (New York: Putnam, 1977), 209

6. Anthony Fellow, "Friendship under Glass: The Story of L.A. *Times* Hatchet Man and Upton Sinclair," *Upton Sinclair Quarterly* 11:7, August 1978, 3. The Ainsworth apartment was crowded with mementos of Sinclair's candidacy.

7. Mitchell, *Campaign of Century*, 561. Shortly after the election, at a Beverly Hills party, Irving Thalberg confessed that he had created the fake newsreels.

8. Ibid., 495, based on *Los Angeles Daily News*, November 3, 1934

9. *Pasadena Post*, November 3, 1934

from *EPIC Answers*

1934

WITHIN WEEKS OF its publication, the pamphlet *I, Governor of California, and How I Ended Poverty: a True Story of the Future* was the best-selling book in California; within a few months, sales topped ninety thousand. In his introduction to a 1994 reissue of Sinclair's *I, Candidate*, James Gregory explained:

> Sinclair was unmatched in his ability to bring ideas down to the level of common sense...for hundreds of thousands of modestly educated Californians, his self-presentation as teacher-with-all-the answers was powerful and self-affirming. He was the teacher, but he taught that they were the experts.[1]

Sinclair followed *I, Governor of California* with an elaboration on the plan, *EPIC Answers*, based on questions from audiences. He centered his campaign on groups of citizens who had been disenfranchised: small property owners, the unemployed, the poor, seniors, widows, and the disabled. Since all the major newspapers ignored his campaign (the *Los Angeles Times* denounced Sinclair's "maggot-like horde" of supporters), supporter Aileen Barnsdall paid for radio time over national hook-ups until Sinclair's followers began publishing the *EPIC News,* which was sold for five cents a copy and achieved a weekly distribution of over one million copies.

Los Angeles County was the center of the EPIC movement; over eight hundred EPIC clubs were formed, most of them in or around Los Angeles. Journalist and historian Carey McWilliams later commented, "Nothing quite like the EPIC campaign in 1934 had ever occurred in American politics."[2] McWilliams described the campaign as one of the most successful experiments in mass education ever performed, with Sinclair's pamphlets exhibiting "matchless skill, lucidity and brilliance."[3]

What is fascinating about *EPIC Answers* is the simplicity and the directness with which Sinclair describes his plan. Nearly every kind of Californian could find her or himself discussed in this pamphlet: workingmen, farmers, clerical workers, businessmen, teachers, doctors, lawyers, artists, clergymen, technicians, salesmen, insurance men, state employees, public utility employees, women, students, the unemployed, capitalists, the elderly, homeowners, and "criminals, racketeers, grafters, etc." The proposals that Sinclair brilliantly assembled still lie before us, a living blueprint for the transformation of our state.

Notes

1. Upton Sinclair, *I, Candidate* (Berkeley: University of California Press, 1994), xv

2. Carey McWilliams, "The Politics of Utopia" in *Fool's Paradise* (Berkeley: Heyday Books, 2001), 65

3. Ibid., 66

FIRST, AS BRIEFLY as possible, what is the EPIC plan? What does it offer to all persons, high and low, rich and poor, old and young, men and women and children?

EPIC proposes to End Poverty In California; the name being derived from the first letters of these four words. The people of our State find themselves in the fifth year of a depression; and if our analysis is correct, this is a permanent crisis. It will not pass so long as the present system endures, and we in the United States have to deal with a permanently unemployed group of not less than twelve million. Including dependents, this means one-fourth of our population. If three-fourths have to carry one-fourth upon their backs, it means bankruptcy for cities, counties, states, and nation.

Previous crises have come and gone. They were caused by the fact that we had overproduced what are known as consumption goods; that is to say, food and clothing, the things we use up in a short time. When they are used up, industry revives again. But the present crisis is caused by overproduction of "capital goods"—that is to say, the means of producing. We have too many steel mills, oil wells, coal mines, automobile factories. These things do not wear out or rust away, and if we wait for this to happen, our unemployed will starve to death.

What causes overproduction? The fact that the wealth of our country has become concentrated in a few hands. Great trusts control prices and cause the profits to flow to them, while farmers and workers are unorganized and compete against one another, beating down the price of what they have to sell. Machines and inventions enable us to turn out enormous quantities of goods, but the farmers and workers do not get enough money to buy these goods back, hence overproduction, which should, really, be called underconsumption.

A few persons own the great industries, and the rest owe the debts. These debts have piled up until all the profits earned in the country are not enough to pay them. This spells bankruptcy for the people, and ultimately for the Government, which gets its income by taxing the people. The United States Government is now making a desperate effort to increase purchasing power, pouring out two billion dollars per month. But this procedure adds to the amount of the debt and makes the condition worse than ever. The next step is inflation, which does not end poverty and unemployment, but ruins the middle class, and leads to attempted revolt, followed by Fascism, as we have seen in Italy, Germany, and Austria.

In our State of California we have now more than a million persons dependent upon public charity for their existence. Many of our counties are already bankrupt. Our State will be more than a hundred million dollars "in the hole" by the end of 1934, and bankruptcy has only been averted by the Federal Government stepping in to take the burden of feeding the hungry. The Federal Government is now supporting the banks, the insurance companies, the railroads, the great industrial corporations; the home-owners, the farmers, the veterans, the unemployed. Bankruptcy for the Federal Government is only a question of months.

To this problem there can be but one solution. It is necessary to put the unemployed at productive labor. A million people in California must be made self-sustaining. They must have access to the land to grow their own food; they must have access to the factories to produce their own clothing and building materials, out of which to make their own homes. We must take them off the backs of the little tax-payers, and stop forcing the latter out of their homes and off their ranches. There must be prompt action, for the crisis is desperate and the next breakdown may lead to attempts at revolt and civil war.

Already the Government is groping its way toward this solution: setting up a furniture factory for unemployed miners in West Virginia; undertaking mass production in the Tennessee Valley; entering into an arrangement with the people of the Virgin Islands, whereby it undertakes the production of sugar and rum and divides the profits with the workers; proposing farm homesteads for the superfluous workers of the great cities.

If the people of all the forty-eight States of this Union sit down and wait for the Federal Government to save them, we shall have such a bureaucracy as the world has never seen. The EPIC plan proposes that the people of California shall have the enterprise and courage to do something for themselves. We have many millions of acres of the most fertile land, and the best climate in the world. We have skilled agricultural workers and machinery, and certainly we can grow our own food. Also we have the factories, equipped with great machines. Many of these factories stand idle, or are running on half time. We have the men who know how to manage them and to work the machines. We can turn out practically all of our basic necessities, and make plenty and comfort for all.

The destitute people cannot get land or factories or raw materials for themselves. This can only be done by the credit of the State. The EPIC plan proposes that the State shall purchase the idle land and factories at the present bankruptcy prices, and shall immediately institute a State system of production and exchange, whereby the unemployed may produce what they consume.

The "subsistence homesteads" now proposed as a solution of the problem constitute a step backward. When men live on small farms and produce only what they themselves consume, they can never escape poverty and drudgery. Modern production is mass production, both on farms and in factories. It requires great tracts of land, costly machinery, and expert direction.

The EPIC plan proposes that the State of California shall set up land colonies in which the unemployed farm workers shall live and produce the food required by the million destitute persons in our State. Operating thus upon a large scale, the farm workers can live in what will amount to new villages, with all the advantages of modern civilization: kitchens and cafeterias operated by the community, a social hall with opportunities for recreation, a church, a school-house, a store, a library, a motion picture theatre, etc. Living thus, the people will have the benefits of mass production by machinery; they will have the advantages of country life without its loneliness and backwardness.

The factories will be great productive units owned and managed by the State. There also will be social buildings with kitchens, cafeterias, lecture halls, libraries, etc. The State will maintain a system of distribution, whereby the food is brought into the cities and the manufactured products are taken out to the land colonies, and all the products of the system are made available at cost. Those who produce will receive the full social value of their product, so they will be able to buy what they have produced, and for the first time consumption will balance production. There can be no overproduction in such a system; when the system produces a surplus, the people will be on a vacation instead of out of a job. They will own the surplus.

Inside the system, payment will be a form of scrip or labor money, a simple accounting system. A man works four hours, and receives a credit, say, of ten dollars, and with this credit he is entitled to buy ten dollars' worth of whatever goods the system has to sell.

Of course there are some things which we cannot produce in California: coffee, for example, and postage stamps. The system will have to purchase these things with United States money, and to get this money it will have to sell a certain portion of the goods outside. We shall have to ship oranges, walnuts, beans, oil to Chicago or New York or London, and receive credit for these goods.

In order to purchase the land and factories and start the system going, the State of California will have to issue bonds. It was planned to ask the people of California, who have more than three billion dollars in private banks, to withdraw a small part of this money and buy the bonds of the State. But since the EPIC plan was put out, the Federal Government has made plain its willingness to support productive enterprises undertaken by responsible groups, and we feel certain now that if the people vote to End Poverty In California, the Federal Government will help them by taking the bonds.

It must be made clear that a loan made to buy the means of production is an entirely different thing from one made to buy goods and give them away. The former may be called "a loan to end loans." Production with modern machinery can be done upon an enormous scale, and when we once get our State production system going, and make our people comfortable and safe, we can set aside a part of our product, sell it outside and pay off our bonds. When this has been done the State factories and land colonies will become self-governing institutions, operating under charters from the state, as our cities and towns do at the present time. This is Democracy applied to industry.

At every meeting where this plan is discussed, someone arises and asks: Why produce more goods when we have already produced more than we can consume? The answer is, because what we have now produced belongs to private owners, and in the effort to purchase it the State is being driven into bankruptcy. That which the people do not own is of no use to the people and might as well not exist. It is proposed that the unemployed shall produce food which they will be able to eat, and clothing which they will be able to wear, without paying any tribute to private owners.

People ask how long it will take to put such a system into effect. The answer is two-fold. As an economic problem the solution could be immediate. We have the land, we have the factories, and we have the people ready to go to work tomorrow. The only real problem is a political one—that of getting power. We cannot have a primary election before August 28, 1934. We cannot have a general election before November 6, 1934. The newly elected Governor cannot take office until January 1, 1935. Since the present Government is too stupid and too corrupt to do anything to help the people, they have to starve along through 1934. The EPIC movement represents their resolve to stop starving as early as possible in 1935.

The rest of the program represents their resolve to correct the inequality of wealth which menaces the very life of our society. Our laws have caused the rich to get richer and the poor poorer. It is proposed to reverse this process.

People are now losing their homes and ranches because they can no longer pay their taxes. The tax system of the State is to be revised, and all homes occupied by the owners and ranches operated by the owners which are assessed at less than $3,000 are to be exempted from taxation. Taxes on the more valuable properties will be graduated, increasing at the rate of one-half of one per cent for each $5,000 of additional valuation.

It is proposed to repeal the State sales tax, which is a tax on poverty, and to raise a portion of the money by means of a State tax upon stock exchange transactions. New York State imposes a tax of 4 cents per share on stock transfers, and there is no reason why California could not do the same. It is estimated that a million shares change hands in our State every gambling day. Let Wall Street pay the sales tax!

Next it is proposed to impose a State income tax. In the United States today an income of $25,000 per year pays 10%. In England, France, and Germany, such an income pays 30% to 40% So there is ample margin for a graduated State income tax. It is also proposed to increase the State inheritance tax in the higher brackets, taking 50% of those great fortunes which are unearned and which are a menace to our society.

Finally, it is proposed to impose a graduated tax upon idle and unused land. Our cities and towns are ringed around with vacant lots held by speculators. If a person owns a lot assessed at not more than $1,000, and wishes to build a home upon that lot, there will be a State building loan fund to make this possible. But persons who are holding large tracts of land out of use will be taxed for it, the tax being graduated according to the valuation held by each individual.

It is also proposed to include a tax on privately owned public utility corporations and banks, which are shamefully undertaxed at present.

The remainder of the EPIC program has to do with those persons who are unable to work. It promises that needy persons over sixty years of age who have lived three years within the State shall receive a pension of $50 per month. It promises the same for the blind and disabled, and for the widowed mothers of dependent children. If there are more than two children, it proposes to add $25 per month for each additional child.

Such is the EPIC plan. Let us now consider what this plan will do for various important groups in our community. We shall take the more numerous groups, and gradually work down to the smaller ones.

Workingmen
The life of the workingman in modern times is conditioned by one fact—that he is competing in a world from which competition has been largely abolished. The workingman competes for the job, and the lowest bidder gets it. Therefore real wages, the purchasing power of the worker, can never increase very much, except in time of war. Efforts are being made to correct this situation by the NRA. These efforts have failed, and will always fail so long as there exists a mass of unemployed workers on the market, bidding for the jobs.

If the EPIC plan is put into effect in California, this condition will be changed for the first time in modern civilization. If the unemployed are taken off the labor market, wages will immediately go up. The workers will earn the right to organize, and can win strikes, and thus reverse the process which has impoverished them and enriched the big employers, the bankers and the speculators.

Under the EPIC plan the worker will always have the alternative of coming into the State system. If the State system produces generously and gives the products to the workers, more and more workers will demand entrance to this system and will secure it.

In the State factories the workers will be free to work as many hours as they please. Of course such an arrangement will have to be within reason. If a man agrees to come and tend a machine at certain hours, he will have to come or lose his job. But there is no reason why one man cannot work three hours a day if he wants to, and another man work eight hours if he wants to. It depends upon how much money each man wishes to earn and spend. Machines can be worked in seven-hour shifts—three shifts per day—and all will have equal interest in speeding up production, because all will be sharing in the benefits of such production.

Certain kinds of labor in California are migratory. Fruit has to be picked at certain seasons and it has to be canned in a rush as soon as it has been picked. In a State system conducted by the workers for their own benefit, such work will be in the nature of a holiday excursion. Provision will be made for moving families from place to place. There will be comfort and recreation for all, schools for the children, everything that is needed to turn work into a pleasure.

So long as the factories are in debt to the State, the State will have to manage them and see that production is achieved. Once the workers have paid off the bonds, they become free citizens of industry, living in a self-governing community, choosing their own managers and officials and determining their own way of life by democratic consent. They maintain, out of their own earnings, sick and accident benefit funds. They have control over social and cultural life, churches, schools, theatres, libraries, concert halls, research laboratories, sports and recreations. They are at liberty to grow their own food on nearby land; or, under the State system, they may exchange their factory products for food grown in the land colonies.

The above statement represents the principles of Democracy applied to industry. The EPIC Plan declares that if government of the people, by the people, and for the people is good in the field of politics, it is equally good where the people earn their daily bread and produce the necessities of their lives. EPIC declares that it is up to a free self-governing Democracy to solve the problems of production and distribution in a manner which grants justice to all and allows to each the utmost freedom compatible with the rights of others.

Farmers

The farmers of California are producing in competition with one another; but when they ship their goods to market, they deal with railroads, trade associations, and a Wall Street system which have learned to cooperate. The farmer is taxed not merely by the State, but by middlemen and speculators, railroads and trucking corporations, advertising men, insurance agents—so on through a long list of parasites who stand between producer and consumer. So it happens that a head of cabbage for which the farmer is paid a fraction of a cent will be sold at retail for ten cents. Prices are so high that the consumers have not the money to buy the goods, and so the farmer has no market. In the effort to keep up prices the Federal Government is now reducing production, the very apex of economic folly.

How can the EPIC plan help the farmer out of his difficulties? The following summary is taken from the book I, Governor of California:

1. Farms assessed at less than $3,000 would be exempt from taxes.
2. As an immediate emergency measure, the State would purchase farm products at wholesale prices, for distribution to the unemployed.
3. Wherever the State was in a position to use produce, it would be accepted for taxes.
4. In parts of the State where all the good land was under cultivation, the State would enter into arrangements with working farmers for the taking of their produce in exchange for credit at the State stores.
5. Entrance into the State System by any farmer would be voluntary. At the beginning the State would work out a trial plan, under which farmers could operate their land for the State on a share basis.
6. The purpose of EPIC would be to see that working farmers, knowing their business and operating it competently, should have the advantage of good soil, machinery, fertilizer, seed, and crop insurance, and have an assured market. Products would be exchanged with the nearest factory workers who produced what the farmers needed, the State acting as a friendly agent to speed the transaction and maintain just prices; the savings in the process coming from the elimination of bankers, brokers, speculators, commission men, insurance agents, advertisers, and all the apparatus of Wall Street.

The first question the farmer asks about EPIC is the question already answered in connection with the factories—why produce more when we cannot consume what we already have? The answer is because the goods now produced can only reach the consumer through the channels of the profit system, and that system of blind competition has raised prices to such an extent that the food products cannot be consumed, but are left to rot on the ground or dumped into the ocean.

I point out to the California farmers that these conditions now exist and were not made by the EPIC plan. The small farmer is being forced out of existence or reduced to a condition of serfdom. The banks are getting his land, and he becomes a tenant, no longer having any interest in the land or motive for taking care of it. Every year he sinks deeper into debt, and what has the present system to offer him?

Under the new system the State will be opening up great land colonies, and workers and managers who understand production will be needed and called for. The farmer who comes into the State system will have the use of the best land and machinery, and when he has produced food he will have a guaranteed market. The factory workers will be turning out manufactured goods to be delivered to the stores and made available to the farmers in the land colonies. Instead of working from dawn to darkness, as does the farmer of today, he will work not more than an eight-hour day at a good salary. He will become a civil servant with a dignified status and security in his job so long as he works efficiently and honorably. He will no longer be living in isolation, but will be a member of a civilized community with all the cultural advantages of a town—but a town without exploitation.

How can such things be possible? The answer is by the saving of all the waste involved in the competitive and speculative handling of foods. The State will have its own trucking system, its own insurance system, its own guaranteed markets and known demand. If the goods are canned, or packed, the State will not have to send salesmen around looking for purchasers, nor will it have to spend tens of millions of dollars advertising its various brands. The banks and Wall Street will be frozen out and the profiteers and gamblers will not be taking their toll out of every cabbage leaf.

Of course no farmer is compelled to enter the State system. If he wants to wait a while and see what happens, he may do so. If he is operating a ranch assessed at less than $3,000—which means a much higher market value—he will be exempt from taxes. Under the system of tax graduation proposed by EPIC, a farm will have to be valued at $15,000 to $20,000 before the rate of taxation will become higher than at present. Also, of course, the farmer will receive the benefit of old age pensions and of the other pensions proposed for all.

The farmers of America have not been told about what is going on in Russia, and few of them realize that under the new system of collective farming, the Soviet Union produced last year a crop more than ten per cent larger than any in its history. A new crop is being sown as this pamphlet goes to press, and if the same results are achieved, it means the end of small-scale farming all over the world; for with their enormous surplus the Russians will destroy the world markets. The real meaning of our national efforts to curtail production of wheat, corn, and cotton is that we are drawing back into our own shell and abandoning the export field to the new system of collective production and state monopoly of markets. Soviet Russia is now the first country in the world in the production of tractors and agricultural machinery. Small-scale farming is dead; and for how long will the farmers of California shut their eyes to this transformation, the most significant in the history of the world?...

Business Men

The first thing to make clear to the small business man is that at present he is being squeezed out of existence. The big trusts and chain stores and chain banks and Wall Street manipulators have got him in a vise. When the State system gets under way, he will find himself gazing at it longingly. The EPIC administrators will say to him as follows:

Your activities are full of waste and futility; you are part of a dying system. Here in our new system we are producing for the benefit of all. We need administrators and advisers of every sort. We offer you a reasonable salary, shorter hours, useful work to do, a guaranteed market—no strikes, graft, racketeers, or adulteration of products. We offer you opportunity to do your best work, and the satisfaction of knowing that you are serving everybody and living up to the best ideals you can conceive. We offer you security of tenure and a pension in your old age. If you prefer to work on the outside, that is all right with us—you will have old-age pensions just the same, and if your home is small it will be exempt from taxation. Do not oppose us, but let us try this new experiment, and if it works, the door will be open for you at any time you care to come in.

Teachers

Public school teachers are now suffering from the graft of politicians and the bankruptcy into which the whole State is drifting. The teachers' own figures this winter show more than two million children of elementary school age being denied education in the United States because the counties are bankrupt and cannot pay the teachers or heat the school buildings. Other millions of school children are on half time for the same reason.

Under a State system of production, teachers in schools will no longer be starved for the benefit of private profit-takers. Their pupils will be able to study because they will come to school well nourished. A progressive and open-minded regime, no longer under the control of big business greed and political graft, will offer opportunities for expansion and experiment in education. A free society in a period of growth will honor teachers as the guardians of the future, and the profession will take the place of honor formerly assigned to bankers and Wall Street speculators.

The teachers in the State system will have security of tenure, and their pensions will be raised. They will have opportunities of recreation, and of outdoor work without loss of status. There is now what is known as Commonwealth College at Mena, Arkansas, where teachers and pupils work part time in the classroom and part time at physical work. Such an arrangement is difficult in our present class society, but it is manifestly a sensible one, and may become popular in a public system of production.

EPIC will not interfere with private teachers and those who are able to earn their way independently. To such teachers the plan offers the same advantages which have been specified in the section for clerical workers: competition by the unemployed being removed, higher pay will be obtainable; there will be exemption from taxation of small homes, the opportunity to build homes; old-age pensions and other benefits which EPIC holds out to all.

Doctors

Under the word "doctor" we include all practitioners of the healing art, dentists, nurses, hospital employees, druggists, etc. Such persons are having a hard time at present. Many doctors get their pay, if any, in the form of loads of wood and sacks of potatoes. The EPIC plan will not interfere with private practice, but doctors will be urgently needed in the State system, and will have reasonable salaries, security of tenure, pensions in old age, and will be able to help anyone who is ill, and not have the painful experience of having to dun the poor for money. They will be able to give advice and have it taken—instead of knowing, as they know today, that they are advocating a nourishing diet to persons who can only afford starch and lard.

The effects of poverty on human health are known to every intelligent health worker. What it means is that the great mass of scientific knowledge is unused. We know about fresh air and sunshine but we keep the people in slums. We know a lot about vitamins but our children grow up stunted by malnutrition. Insanity is on the increase among us, due to the strain of blind competition. Research is being starved. Drugs are adulterated for private profit. The answer to all this is socialized medicine, with true scientists in charge of public health, free for the first time to put their knowledge into effect....

Artists

Under the present system all cultural activities serve the rich. Many painters, actors, dramatists, novelists, and musicians cater directly to the rich, glorifying their lives and feeding their prejudices. Others serve exploiters of art; they cater to the ignorant, and keep them in ignorance, feeding their lowest tastes. In neither form of activity can a creative artist have any true pride.

EPIC proposes the building of a new social life, and will make possible a new social art. There will be group interests to be served, and collective ideals to be glorified. The EPIC movement has issued a leaflet prepared by some of the leading artists, musicians, and other cultural workers of California, setting forth what this movement can do for the arts; State theatres and orchestras for the entire population, and cultural activities of all sorts in the land colonies and the publicly owned factory centers. Our workers have very little true culture at present, because they are serfs of industry, exploited both physically and materially. They have little leisure and no security; their lives are dull and their tastes crude. But under a free system, owned and managed by the useful workers of both hand and brain, culture for all will become possible—and in fact a certainty, because modern machinery will so shorten hours that society will be driven in self-defense to teach the workers forms of recreation which are helpful and constructive.

Clergymen

The minister of religion now is necessarily an ineffectual man; he preaches the fatherhood of God and the brotherhood of man, while he sees that everybody is practicing exploitation, greed, hatred, and strife. He has to shut his eyes to the week-day activities of his parishioners.

Under the EPIC system the status of religion will be unchanged. The churches are free voluntary groups supported by those who are interested in them. Whatever churches the people in the land colonies want, they will have. The change which EPIC will make for the clergyman is that which will take place in the minds and hearts of his parishioners, due to a new economic way of life. For the first time in history it will be possible to practice the Golden Rule in daily affairs. For the first time it will be possible for love to prevail on week-days, and people may listen to the minister on Sunday and really know what he is talking about. The EPIC plan was foretold twenty-five hundred years ago by the prophet Isaiah: "And they shall build houses and inhabit them; and they shall plant vineyards and eat the fruit of them. They shall not build and another inhabit; they shall not plant and another eat."...

Insurance Men

...Under a State system, insurance becomes a superfluity, because the State has ample capital to cover its own losses. Insurance men, an educated and thinking group, will be welcomed as administrators under the EPIC system; or they may continue to serve the private system and await developments....

Public Utility Employees

At present the public utilities pass on all taxes to the consumer. They have been able to do this because of their control of political parties—taking the money of the consumer and using it to subsidize political bosses, and thus protect their ability to exploit the public. EPIC will enable the people to break the hold of the public utility corporations over the State Railroad Commission. And when the profits of the public utilities are limited, they will have less money for graft, and will make less opposition to a program of public ownership. In the meantime, the plan will free the public utility employees from fear of losing their jobs, and enable them, with all other workers, to demand higher pay. They will receive all the benefits of pensions, tax exemption, homebuilding fund, etc., listed for all under EPIC.

Women

The EPIC system offers to women independence for the first time. Work will be plentiful and there will be many kinds of work adapted to the skill and strength of women. There will be maternity allowances, mothers' pensions, old-age pensions. The exemption of small homes and ranches from taxation will aid a majority of the women of California. Also they will be aided as consumers through the providing of goods at cost in the stores. Women who want to marry and rear families will know that their husbands have permanent jobs. Women who work to help support their children will have the help of creches, nurseries, and kindergartens in all State factories and land colonies. Women who wish to live independent lives can always find honorable occupations, and thus for the first time it will be possible to abolish prostitution and commercialized vice....

Unemployed

To those now unemployed and begging for a chance to earn a living, EPIC is a new world, built for them and managed by them. Instead of being outcasts, they become free citizens in a self-governing and self-sustaining community, and so long as they render honest service there will be no way for them to lose their rights as industrial freemen. But everyone in the State system will have to work. Charity will be done away with. The State, offering work, will pay no doles to able-bodied persons, and begging will become both a misdemeanor and a public disgrace.

Everyone working in the State system will be free to select the kind of work he wishes to do—provided, of course, that he is competent to do it. He will be permitted, within reason, to work as many hours as he pleases. It is nobody's affair but his own how much wealth he produces and enjoys. Some will live simply and have their time free for study and recreation. Others like to drive expensive automobiles. Every person will know that he has earned what he spends, and will thus keep his self-respect and the esteem of his fellows.

Capitalists

At first glance it may sound humorous to recommend to capitalists a system of graduated State income taxes, inheritance taxes, and land taxes. But it is a fact that the owning class will benefit under EPIC, not merely spiritually but materially. To be able to make great sums of money is not all the capitalist has to think about; he likes to be able to keep what he makes. But under the present system he can have no certainty of keeping anything. His competitors are trying to put him out of business, and racketeers are preying upon him by a thousand devices. At present our State and Nation are headed for bankruptcy and inflation, which will wipe out large groups of capitalists—all those who depend upon investments. Wars and revolutions loom in the future, and it is a literal fact that there is no security for any kind of ownership in our present collapsing world. No man can hand on a fortune to his widow and children with certainty that they will enjoy the fruits of his labor.

It should mean something to the rich man to be able to live in a world where kidnapers are not threatening to steal his children, and where burglars are not breaking into his home at night. It ought to mean something to a big business administrator to have the chance to build an honest world, in which he is making plenty and security, not merely for himself but for everybody in his State. The intellectual and moral advantages of EPIC are extended to every member of the community, and especially to the rich, because under our present system these persons have the advantages of knowledge and training, and will be needed in a cooperative world—provided that they are willing to cooperate.

Our society is in rapid transition, and the rich have to make a choice of vital import to them. Blind resistance to social forces leads inevitably to tragedy; and we urge our propertied classes to manifest intelligence and humanity, and lend their help in a peaceful transition to the new era by popular consent. What else does Democracy mean?...

Home Owners
Those who already own small homes in California will, under the EPIC plan, stop losing them to the money-lenders and the banks. There will be an end of nuisance taxes and the activities of loan sharks. The effect of graduated taxes will be felt only by the owners of large and expensive homes. If you have a lot and want to build a home, there will be a State fund for this purpose, and the total cost to you will be less than you are paying the landlord for rent. The

tax on unused land will make building lots cheap. In the land colonies you can rent a house built by the State, or you can get a lot upon a long-term tease at low rental and build for yourself any sort of home you want.

EPIC will make it possible for every individual to have the sort of home that he desires. There will be only one restriction, as in every sort of activity—a person must render to the community a service equivalent to the value of the home he builds or rents.

In the cities at present are thousands of vacant apartment houses which have been lost to banks and mortgage holders. To take over these apartment houses and put them upon a cooperative basis, enabling the tenants to purchase a share in them and manage them collectively, is another answer to the housing problem which EPIC would favor.

Criminals, Racketeers, Grafters, etc.
These activities become unnecessary under EPIC, and such persons will have opportunity to engage in productive labor.

———
———

A NUMBER OF questions are regularly asked at EPIC meetings.

Won't there be too many people coming into the State of California if the EPIC plan is a success?

Answer: All persons will bring with them their hands and their heads. They will use their heads to put their hands at work, and will produce the equivalent of what they consume. This will help to make prosperity in California. Being afraid of new people is part of the present profit system, under which jobs are scarce. When we are producing for use, there will be jobs for all.

Can one State carry out such a plan alone?

Answer: California can produce practically everything our people need, and there is nothing to keep us from producing these things, and consuming them.

Will not the plan drive capital out of the State?

Answer: It may drive a few of the capitalists out, and they may take with them their bank accounts and stocks and bonds.

But they will not take the land of California, nor the factories, nor the workers. The latter will go to work on the land and in the factories, and will turn out plenty of wealth for themselves. When the capitalists see how things are going, they will remember the pleasant climate of California, and come back, and perhaps ask to be given some useful work....

Will all workers in the State system be paid alike?

Answer: No, because in that case we should have to assign the workers to the various jobs by compulsion, and we desire as little as possible of that in our community. Let every man choose his job, provided it is one for which he is competent. Attract labor to the various jobs by shifting the compensation slightly, offering higher wages, or what is the same thing, shorter hours, in the jobs found to be less attractive.

Will people not be confused by a conflict of two different systems?

Answer: We are quite accustomed to living under two systems at present. We stop at a privately owned hotel and pay money for our room and meals; but if the hotel catches fire, the publicly owned fire department puts the fire out; if a burglar enters our room, the publicly owned police department protects us. The proprietor of the hotel sends his children to the public schools, etc. All we propose to do in California is to set up one more public body of the sort we now take for granted: the United States Army and Navy, the State Highway Patrol, the county school system, the city water department and garbage collection system....

Will the owning class give up without a struggle?

Answer: We are proposing an orderly and peaceable social change. If the people elect candidates pledged to End Poverty in California, we believe that the Federal Government will see to it that they take office. There is no way to be sure but to try....

Will you be able to control the Legislature?

Answer: All members of the Assembly come up for re-election this fall, but only half of senators are to be elected. This of course will present a problem. If the people cast a sufficiently large vote for EPIC the hold-over senators will hardly dare block our way. If they persist we can recall them; or the Governor will prepare a series of EPIC enactments which can be put through by the method of initiative and referendum. If the people want to End Poverty in California, and will stick by their resolve, the job can be done. No person should be chosen as an EPIC candidate until he has pledged himself to stand by this method of procedure to the end. It is up to us to vindicate the principles of Democracy, and see to it that government of the people, by the people, and for the people does not perish from California.

Where can I learn more about this program?

…As soon as you have a group large enough, call a meeting and a speaker will be sent to you. Understand, the EPIC movement has no campaign funds from corporations, chain banks, or others who expect to benefit at the expense of the useful workers. This is a people's movement, and whatever you do for it you are doing for yourself and not for any of the candidates. The people must assert themselves in this crisis and vindicate the system of Democracy, or that system will perish from California, as it has already perished from the greater part of the continent of Europe.

More than 650 EPIC clubs are already functioning in California, and if you write to Headquarters you may learn the address of the nearest group. Volunteer labor of every sort is needed: writers, speakers, organizers, literature sellers, persons to address envelopes and wrap literature, etc. There is some kind of work for everyone.

The last word of EPIC to the people of California is: IT'S UP TO YOU.

Artifacts of the Campaign
1934

AN ESPECIALLY EXCITING feature of the EPIC campaign was its insistent use of popular culture to reach the public. Imagine a radical candidate presiding over a "grand rodeo" complete with "rough riders," foot races, "acroplanes releasing parachutes," and cowboy bands! When a group of unemployed actors formed an EPIC troupe, Sinclair wrote a play for them titled *Depression Island*, which was performed on June 27, 1934.[1]

EPIC clubs in every community in California sponsored barbecues, picnics, sewing bees, dances, and athletic competitions. Woulden Howell staged an EPIC pageant created by his art students in the Pasadena schools.[2] With a week remaining in the race, Los Angeles supporter Frank Hoyt circulated a pamphlet with his own Open Letter to the voters. His memoir of the EPIC campaign describes his blue and white "magic Sinclair button" and the responses it drew. In a department store in Los Angeles, a clerk told him, "All the clerks here are for Sinclair but the boss doesn't know it." A streetcar conductor told him, "If he [Sinclair] isn't elected, we're sunk." A young man in Long Beach told him that he'd been told by his corporate employers that "to keep our jobs we must vote for Merriam and carry his stickers on our automobiles. There are sixty of us in the department who are using the stickers, but we are all voting for Sinclair."[3]

The depth of the support for Sinclair was such that he received more votes in the primary than his six opponents put together. Sinclair's candidacy touched people's lives to the extent that an unemployed Los Angeles couple who became parents of a baby boy on primary day, the Marshaws, named him Upton Sinclair Marshaw.[4]

Notes

1. Upton Sinclair, *Depression Island* (Pasadena, Calif.: Upton Sinclair, 1935). Sinclair also hoped to see it produced as a film.

2. Betty Hanson, *Upton Sinclair: Political Campaigner* (*Uppie Speaks* 2:2, March 1978), 5

3. Frank Hoyt, "The Magic Sinclair Button," *Upton Sinclair Quarterly* v:2, June 1981, 3-5

4. *Los Angeles Examiner*, August 29, 1934

Hundreds of thousands of these "dollars" printed in red ink were circulated throughout California.

I, GOVERNOR OF CALIFORNIA

And How I Ended Poverty

A True Story of the Future

BY

UPTON SINCLAIR

This is not just a pamphlet.

This is the beginning of a Crusade.

A Two-Year Plan to make over a State.

To capture the Democratic primaries and use an old party for a new job.

The EPIC plan:

(E)nd (P)overty (I)n (C)alifornia!

The Best Selling Book in the History of California
150,000 in Four Months

PRICE 20 CENTS

END POVERTY LEAGUE 1501 SOUTH GRAND AVE. LOS ANGELES, CALIFORNIA
INCORPORATED
(ADDRESS ALL LETTERS AS ABOVE)

Sinclair presented his vision in this pamphlet that became the principal organizing tool of the campaign. He narrated the story backward from the fictional future of 1938, in the style of Edward Bellamy's 1888 utopian novel, *Looking Backward*.

The bee was the symbol of the EPIC movement; the slogan "I Produce—I Defend" referred to Sinclair's concept of "production for use," which would turn fields over to farmers and factories to workers.

Everywhere that EPIC clubs met, people sang this and other songs to strengthen their commitment to the campaign.

"End Poverty in All America!"—the official song of Sinclair's campaign.

I, Candidate for Governor: And How I Got Licked

Chapter XL, 1935

WHEN ALL THE BALLOTS were counted, incumbent Merriam received one million votes to Sinclair's nine hundred thousand. Sinclair had received twice the number of votes of any previous Democratic candidate in California.[1] Although Sinclair was defeated by the negative campaign waged against him, fifty EPIC-backed candidates won races for the state legislature. It was EPIC that established the Democratic Party as a progressive force in California.[2] State Chairman Culbert Olson wrote, "Upton Sinclair has re-founded the Democrats in this state, and we take up where he left off."[3] In 1936, Olson beat Merriam for governor by over two hundred thousand votes and Sheridan Downey, Sinclair's former running mate, was elected to the U.S. Senate. Years later, Carey McWilliams saw the slogans of the EPIC Campaign "painted on rocks in the desert, carved in trees in the forest, and scrawled on the walls of labor camps in the San Joaquin Valley."[4]

But in 1934, Mary Craig wept with relief at the news of her husband's defeat.[5] Sinclair himself felt that he had literally dodged a bullet. A friend had told him that on election night, a businessman she knew had written out his will, stuck a pistol in his pocket, and set out for a radio station where Sinclair was scheduled to speak. If Sinclair had won, the businessman would have shot him dead on the spot.[6] But Sinclair's followers were inconsolable. Lola Dominguez, a twenty-eight-year-old woman from East Los Angeles, drank poison when she heard the election returns on the radio.[7]

Three days after the election, Upton Sinclair started dictating his campaign memoir. Dozens of newspapers purchased the serial rights, and by November 19, the *San Francisco Chronicle* was publishing chapters daily. Sinclair's campaign was, Theodore Dreiser concluded, "the most impressive political phenomenon that America has yet produced."[8]

Notes

1. Greg Mitchell explains that a few days after the election, Will Rogers observed that if Sinclair had only a few more dollars, he would have won. On August 15, 1935, Rogers died in the crash of a small plane. When rescue workers discovered his typewriter, they found the sheet of paper that carried his final message: "Now I must get back to my Democrats." The nation mourned him with the largest display of affection for a public figure since the death of Abraham Lincoln. (Greg Mitchell, *The Campaign of the Century*, New York: Random House, 1992, 565)

2. Sinclair said, "When I talked to Franklin Roosevelt I told him my immediate demands in the EPIC movement...he checked them off on his fingers and said, 'Right, right, right,' and so on. He brought about a great many of those changes." (Ron Gottesman, Interview with Upton Sinclair, Columbia Oral History Project, 61)

3. *EPIC News*, November 12, 1934

4. Carey McWilliams, "The Politics of Utopia," in *Fool's Paradise* (Berkeley: Heyday Books, 2001)

5. Upton Sinclair, *The Autobiography of Upton Sinclair* (New York: Harcourt Brace and World, 1962)

6. Greg Mitchell, Interview with David Sinclair, Columbia Oral History Collection

7. *Los Angeles Herald*, November 7, 1934

8. Theodore Dreiser, "The EPIC Sinclair," *Esquire*, December 1934

———

ELECTION DAY. My wife and I cast our votes in the morning, and I obliged the cameramen and newsreel operators— although feeling certain in my own mind that those shots would never be used.

The rest of the day we stayed at home, expecting to rest; but the telephone kept ringing, with messages from headquarters and other places, where members of our lawyers' committee were carrying on the fight against frauds at the polls. This is an aspect of the campaign which I have not discussed. We knew what was being prepared. We knew that every agency of corruption and intimidation in California had been marshalling its forces for that day. We knew that our voters had been listed for challenge, and that threats against them had caused thousands who were ignorant of their rights to decide that the safest course was to stay at home.

We knew also of the plans for the stuffing of ballot boxes and the turning in of false returns. A series of incidents had occurred, connected with a proposal to bring from New York a group of men who were familiar with these arts. Some of our friends had worked in New York, and explained our purposes; the upshot being that this particular gang decided not to take the Los Angeles money. I was confirmed in my conclusion that I would rather deal with gamblers and the underworld than with the big business crowd which rules our State.

I had the consciousness of having done my best, and was prepared to take serenely what I knew was coming. I expected a worse defeat than I got—having relied too much upon the *Literary Digest*. A few friends came to our home that evening and we listened over the radio. In the first precinct that reported, soon after the polls closed, Merriam was leading me by four to one, and I thought it was going to be that way straight through. But soon it became evident that we had got an enormous vote, and for a while there seemed a possibility that when the industrial districts of Los Angeles were heard from, we might get out in front.

I won't reveal the names of our friends or how they behaved. Suffice it to say that my wife and I were the least unhappy persons in that company, and we were in the strange position where it didn't seem decent to say how we felt. If we smiled at the funeral, what would the other mourners think? But in my heart were things such as this: I can drive my own car again! I can go and take my walks! I can sleep with my windows open!

Presently we had to bundle into our cars and make a tour of the radio stations. The National Broadcasting Company had prepared a miracle; at ten-thirty I was to have five minutes in which to tell the audiences of ninety-two stations how I felt about being defeated for Governor of California. The alleged Federal regulations were forgotten; I didn't have to "file copy," and was free to say what I pleased. Half an hour later the same privilege was extended by the Columbia chain, sixty-seven stations, if I remember. And then, at eleven-fifteen, KNX turned over its fifty thousand watts for me to use as long as I pleased.

At the first of these stations Governor Merriam preceded me. We were supposed to speak from the same room, but this honor I refused. I have never cultivated the arts of pretense, and I didn't care to exchange courtesies with such a man. I meant to speak out of my heart that night.

I was told afterwards that many people considered that I showed myself "a poor sport," "a bad loser," and so on. I was prepared for that. I was not playing a game, and there was no "sport" about it; I was voicing the anguish of a million suffering people in California. I was fighting for their rights, and making no truce with their ene-mies. The election had been won by a campaign of character assas-sination, and Merriam had permitted that campaign, and now was profiting by it.

I owed him no favors, and showed him none. I conceded that the election had been stolen, and that we would try to prove the theft. I said that the EPIC movement was going right on. We would show the people how Merriam failed to carry out his campaign promises, and in six months we would start a movement to recall him. We would make our preparations to spread our End Poverty League over the entire United States, and we would not quit until every man and woman in our country who needed work had been given the right to work and enjoy the product.

People who heard me said that I was menacing that night; one said that I "roared." Maybe so. I have told in these pages what I had endured for six months or more. I felt that a crime had been com-mitted, not against me, but against the people. It was their rage that I was voicing, not my own. The ruling classes of America were lis-tening to me—certainly the ruling classes of California were, and I told them: "We will hang the threat of a recall as a sword over Merriam's head." Maybe that accounts for the fact that the new Governor-elect has not yet forgotten his campaign promises, a whole month afterward!

I had no chance to visit any of our headquarters that night, but I was told of dreadful scenes. Men and women broke down and wept when the certainty of our defeat became apparent. I know of women who cried the whole night through, and doubtless there were thousands. I know of one suicide, and at least one other attempt. The million-and-a-quarter hungry and desolate people had been hoping for deliverance, and suddenly their hopes were dashed...

To finish the story of the election and its results: the official figures show that Merriam received 1,138,000, I received 879,000, and Haight 302,000. It thus appears that Merriam is a minority Governor by a small margin. He and his masters will not fail to make note of that fact.

A day or so after the election, the Pasadena *Post* stated editorially that I had charged frauds on election night without having had any opportunity to know whether or not any frauds had been committed. Of course, the editors of the Pasadena *Post* didn't mind making charges against me without having had any opportunity to know what I had known. I had been getting reports all day long from people who themselves had been witnesses to the frauds. A few days after the election there was put into my hands a stack of affidavits from the victims and witnesses of frauds. There were reports not only from Los Angeles County, but from all over the State. An official of San Francisco remarked blandly in my hearing that no frauds had been committed in that city; whereupon Ralph Wakefield, our San Francisco manager, replied, "We have one precinct in San Francisco in which three votes were counted for Sinclair, and we have so far the affidavits of forty registered voters in that precinct who voted for Sinclair."...

We elected Culbert L. Olson, State Senator from Los Angeles County, and we elected most of our assemblymen from Los Angeles County, and others from various places. Altogether, we shall have nearly thirty EPIC men in the assembly. It is impossible to tell exactly, because some are Democrats whom we endorsed, and we cannot tell in advance whether they will "stick"; but certainly we have enough to constitute a powerful bloc in the next legislature. We shall bring our measures forward and force them to a vote, and keep our plan to End Poverty before the people of California. The political life of this State is going to be different from now on; the reactionaries will not take everything for granted!

Recommended Reading

Ahouse, John
Upton Sinclair: A Descriptive, Annotated Bibliography
(Los Angeles: Arundel Press, 1994)

Bloodworth, William
Upton Sinclair (Boston: Twayne Publishers, 1977)

Dell, Floyd
Upton Sinclair: A Study in Social Protest (New York: George
Doran, 1927)

Geduld, Harry and Ronald Gottesman
*Sergei Eisenstein and Upton Sinclair: The Making and
Unmaking of* Que Viva Mexico! (Bloomington: University
of Indiana, 1970)

Gottesman, Ronald
Upton Sinclair: An Annotated Checklist (Kent, Ohio: Kent
State University Press, 1973)

Hahn, Robert, ed.
The Upton Beall Sinclair Centenary Journal (California State
University, Los Angeles, September 1978)

Herms, Dieter
Upton Sinclair: Literature and Social Reform (New York:
Peter Lang, 1990)

Mitchell, Greg
The Campaign of the Century (New York: Random House,
1992)

Mookerjee, R. N.
Art for Social Justice: The Major Novels of Upton Sinclair
(Metuchen, N.J.: Scarecrow Press, 1988)

Nakada, Sachiko
    Japanese Empathy for Upton Sinclair (Tokyo: The Central
    Institute, 1990)

Sinclair, Mary Craig
    Southern Belle (New York: Crown Publishers, 1957)

Sinclair, Upton
    American Outpost (New York: Farrar and Rinehart, 1932)
    Another Pamela (New York: Viking Press, 1950)
    The Autobiography of Upton Sinclair (New York: Harcourt
    Brace and World, 1962)
    The Brass Check (Champaign, Ill.: University of Illinois, 2002)
    The Cry for Justice (Philadelphia: The John C. Winston
    Company Publishers, 1915)
    The Cup of Fury (Great Neck, N.Y.: Channel Press, 1956)
    The Gnomobile (Indianapolis: The Bobbs Merrill Company,
    1962)
    The Goslings (Pasadena: Upton Sinclair, 1924)
    I, Candidate for Governor: And How I Got Licked (Berkeley:
    University of California Press, 1994)
    Mental Radio (Charlottesville, Va.: Hampton Roads
    Publishing, 2001)
    The Millennium (New York: Seven Stories Press, 2002)
    My Lifetime in Letters (Columbia, Mo.: University of
    Missouri Press, 1960)
    Oil! (Berkeley: University of California Press, 1997)
    Upton Sinclair Presents William Fox (Los Angeles: Upton
    Sinclair, 1933)
    World's End (New York: Viking Press, 1940)

Stone, Irving
    An Upton Sinclair Anthology (Culver City, Calif.: Murray
    and Gee, 1947)

Yoder, John
    Upton Sinclair (New York: Ungar Publishing, 1975)

Uppie Speaks and the *Upton Sinclair Quarterly* were part of an
effort that spanned 1978 to 1990 to preserve Sinclairiana. Past
issues of both journals can be found in the libraries of several
universities, including: California State University Long Beach;
Columbia University; Cornell University; Hamilton College;
Harvard University; Indiana University; University of California
at Los Angeles, Santa Barbara, and Santa Cruz; University
of Michigan; University of the Pacific; University of Southern
California; University of Southern Illinois at Carbondale;
University of Washington; and at the Huntington Library,
the New York Public Library, and the Library of Congress.

A California Legacy Book

Santa Clara University and Heyday Books are pleased to publish the California Legacy series, vibrant and relevant writings drawn from California's past and present.

Santa Clara University—founded in 1851 on the site of the eighth of California's original twenty-one missions—is the oldest institution of higher learning in the state. A Jesuit institution, it is particularly aware of its contribution to California's cultural heritage and its responsibility to preserve and celebrate that heritage.

Heyday Books, founded in 1974, specializes in critically acclaimed books on California literature, history, natural history, and ethnic studies.

Books in the California Legacy series appear as anthologies, single author collections, reprints of important books, and original works. Taken together, these volumes bring readers a new perspective on California's cultural life, a perspective that honors diversity and finds great pleasure in the eloquence of human expression.

Series editor: Terry Beers
Publisher: Malcolm Margolin
Advisory committee: Stephen Becker, William Deverell, Charles Faulhaber, David Fine, Steven Gilbar, Ron Hansen, Gerald Haslam, Robert Hass, Jack Hicks, Timothy Hodson, James Houston, Jeanne Wakatsuki Houston, Maxine Hong Kingston, Frank LaPena, Ursula K. Le Guin, Jeff Lustig, Tillie Olsen, Ishmael Reed, Alan Rosenus, Robert Senkewicz, Gary Snyder, Dr. Kevin Starr, Richard Walker, Alice Waters, Jennifer Watts, Al Young

Thanks to the English Department at Santa Clara University and to Regis McKenna for their support of the California Legacy series.

Related California Legacy Books

Fool's Paradise: A Carey McWilliams Reader
Foreword by Wilson Carey McWilliams

Mark Twain's San Francisco
Edited by Bernard Taper

Storm
George R. Stewart

The Journey of the Flame
Walter Nordhoff

California: A Study of American Character
Josiah Royce

Eldorado: Adventures in the Path of Empire
Bayard Taylor

Lands of Promise and Despair: Chronicles
of Early California, 1535–1846
Edited by Rose Marie Beebe and Robert M. Senkewicz

Unfinished Message: Selected Works of Toshio Mori
Introduction by Lawson Fusao Inada

And many others.

For more California Legacy titles, events, or other information, please visit www.californialegacy.org. If you would like to be added to the California Legacy mailing list, please send your name, address, phone number, and email address to:

California Legacy Project
English Department
Santa Clara University
Santa Clara, CA 95053

About the Author

Lauren Coodley was born in Los Angeles, where her grandparents settled shortly after Upton Sinclair's arrival. She now lives in Napa with her two children, Nils and Caitlin. She teaches at Napa Community College, specializing in California labor and women's history as well as children's literature. She is the elected president of the faculty and a recipient of the McPherson Distinguished Teaching Award for 2003. She is the author of *Napa: The Transformation of an American Town* (Arcadia Publishing, 2004).